Success
MOTIVATION
for Kids

Preparing Kids for Success In A Negative World

Kenneth Teel

WestBow
PRESS
A DIVISION OF THOMAS NELSON

Copyright © 2011 Kenneth Teel

All rights reserved. No part of this book may be used or reproduced by any means, graphic, electronic, or mechanical, including photocopying, recording, taping or by any information storage retrieval system without the written permission of the publisher except in the case of brief quotations embodied in critical articles and reviews.

WestBow Press books may be ordered through booksellers or by contacting:

WestBow Press
A Division of Thomas Nelson
1663 Liberty Drive
Bloomington, IN 47403
www.westbowpress.com
1-(866) 928-1240

Because of the dynamic nature of the Internet, any web addresses or links contained in this book may have changed since publication and may no longer be valid. The views expressed in this work are solely those of the author and do not necessarily reflect the views of the publisher, and the publisher hereby disclaims any responsibility for them.

Any people depicted in stock imagery provided by Thinkstock are models, and such images are being used for illustrative purposes only.

Certain stock imagery © Thinkstock.

ISBN: 978-1-4497-2150-3 (sc)
ISBN: 978-1-4497-2151-0 (e)

Library of Congress Control Number: 2011912938

Printed in the United States of America

WestBow Press rev. date: 11/17/2011

Table of Contents

Introduction		ix
Prologue		xiii
Forward		xv
Acknowledgements		xix
Chapter 1	Where does success motivation come from?	1
Chapter 2	Parent's critical role in building children's self worth	13
Chapter 3	"Self esteem" – Psychcobabble or gospel?	25
Chapter 4	How does 'authority' interface with success?	40
Chapter 5	Whatever became of 'submission to authority?'	56
Chapter 6	How does child discipline fit into success motivation?	69
Chapter 7	Confronting pride - critical in motivating kids	82
Chapter 8	What about kid's opinions, how much do they count?	94
Chapter 9	How much freedom, when?	102
Chapter 10	Problem solving and motivating kids with seeds of faith	110
Chapter 11	The difference between control and leadership	117
Chapter 12	Embracing forgiveness	126

Children's Bill of Rights	135
The 12 Keys to Success Motivation	136
Ken's Kids	137
Author contact information	141

Success
MOTIVATION
for Kids

Preparing Kids for Success In A Negative World

Introduction

It's been on my heart for several years to write this book and so after seeming endless delays, here it is.

Over the past five decades, our country has struggled to bring freedom and rights to oppressed peoples. Out of its soul-searching and pain, this nation has produced civil rights, women's rights, farmer's rights, gay rights, and even criminal's rights even though not all these rights have an equal basis of legitimacy.

Looking at the over all picture of our culture, I think the segment that has perhaps been neglected, abused, sexualized, traumatized, and mistreated most have been our children. No other group in society today more desperately needs repositioning and support.

The greatest cause before us today is reclaiming our children. This is the most urgent need. The present generation of kids should be given special attention. If there was ever a time to proclaim and reclaim the rights of children - it is now - the hour in which we live.

I believe children have a right to grow up s-l-o-w-l-y. They have a right to be treated with respect. They have a right to be accepted and loved for who they are without being compared to another sibling or expected to perform at some level they are not capable of. I think there are many fine parents and adults who believe this, yet believing is one thing - ***doing*** something about it is an altogether different story.

I believe each and every child is a unique human being, created in the image of God with the stamp of greatness in his or her soul. It's possible for that greatness to be tapped and brought to great heights in every child if given half a chance. It's also possible for that greatness to be smashed, distorted, and laid waste.

Teaching success motivation to children is an urgent issue today. I think everyone ought to be teaching it: parents, teachers, church workers, and anyone else interested in making a difference in children's lives and our future.

The abuse of children is a deep wound in America's side. It's like a festering sore with a thorn imbedded profoundly into the center of it.

My heart has been broken many times over children who have suffered neglect and abuse of every imaginable sort from the very people they were supposed to trust. Too many kids today find themselves caught in a horrific dilemma of desperately wanting and needing love from the very grown-ups who are hurting them irreparably.

Adults who have been raised in dysfunctional families are now raising dysfunctional families of their own. We all know that. The sad fact is, it's not getting any better. Kids in these families are resenting or hating their parents or rebelling against them because their parent's may be acting out their own hurts and distortions of reality on their own kids - innocent victims who neither know how to interpret their hurt correctly or process it in a rational way.

This generation is being launched into life with horrendous handicaps, directly due to wrong thinking, wrong decisions, and wrong actions set against them by the authorities in their lives. It is my hope this book will build a bridge over long held prejudices and traditions which have led to perpetuating the same mistakes over and over again.

This guidebook is dedicated to parents who love their children and desire to love them more. It's also dedicated to parents who know they're not loving their children in the best way possible. It's written in behalf of children around the world with the hope that things will get better. It's also dedicated to *all* adults helping small people around the world everyday become all they can be.

Prologue

When you read some of the ideas in this book you may say, "I knew that." Well, that's good! Now you can apply these ideas! These concepts have been around for a long time. It's my hope you will let them sink in and change the way you've been relating to yourself and others.

Truth often comes to us in disarmingly simple ways. Profound insight changes us because it touches something beyond our intellect. I hope I've reached my goal in this book by making difficult ideas simple. I've tried to be honest, real, and show how the principles work.

I'll be making references to the Bible throughout these pages – the best-selling book of all time. I don't apologize for that. Scripture references give insight into what I'm covering and add credibility to the principles of success motivation. The Bible quotations I've used create a broader perspective than "pop" psychology. They lend further understanding and acceptance of the truths contained in the book. I'm sure you're interested in things that work in the real world. This book is written to that end. All Bible quotations are from the New International Version (NIV) unless otherwise indicated.

I've been amused and somewhat dismayed over the years to read or hear of books with titles such as, <u>101 Ways To Live a Happy Marriage</u>, only to discover a few years later that the author divorced, then remarried and divorced again. Or take the book with the title, <u>How to Lose 100 pounds in 100 Days</u>, written by an author who died from obesity after finishing it.

What's wrong with that picture?

I think it's very difficult to trust anyone these days. It seems very few public figures stick to the truth. There's a lot of exaggerating and fabricating by those in the public eye we've been called to trust. It seems difficult for politicians and those who hold public office to keep information factual. I might add, without character, all the good ideas in the world mean nothing because character *is* the foundation for knowing. Being intelligent is great but if you don't know right from wrong, you are lost, confused, or worse, dangerous.

The ideas shared in this book are practical, real, tried, and their positive effects have been demonstrated through the lives of real people.

At the end of this book I have included a personal glimpse into the lives of some of those people - my own kids - who are grown now. I thought it would be helpful for you to see how the principles of this book actually worked out in real life. I hope you enjoy this section as I struggled with whether or not to include it. I hope it will encourage you in raising your own kids. In the 'ups and downs' and the 'tragic and funny' of raising my kids, God has been incredibly faithful.

Forward

This book is a thoughtful work that is not only applicable to parenting but outlines the principles necessary to succeed in life.

Everyone is a leader. A formal leader is someone with a title. An informal leader is someone who leas others but has not formal position. We're all leaders.

Parenting is nature's ultimate gift of formal leadership. Unlike many other kinds of leadership, the responsibility of this role includes the physical, spiritual, emotional, mental, and financial care of children. Mothers and fathers would agree that parenting is one of life's most daunting challenges. It's a role that requires great leadership, patience, and love.

As the writer reveals, steps for success for children is also an exposition on timeless leadership insights applicable for all ages and in every relationship, no matter the stage of life.

Many of the examples in the book will bring back childhood memories, some of which may be positive and some negative. The principles in the book serve as a compass to guide the reader into self

> *I'm confident that Success Motivation for Children will help you prepare the same bag of tools for your sons and daughters and provide you with a renewed perspective on life.*

discovery and inspire them through the pain and joy to be the best parents and leaders possible. It will help them strive for more meaningful relationships at work, home, church, on the job, and in the community. The world certainly needs a new generation of leaders raised by the values outlined by the author.

As son of the author, a husband and father of three, I've used the principles of success motivation for my own kids and for my own personal challenges. As a USAF officer and enlisted man I used the lessons my dad taught me to help me through the most difficult times.

The lessons outlined in the book concerning authority were particularly useful to me in a military environment which is renowned for being rough. My dad wrestled and boxed in high school and college and was sure to teach us these skills around the age of 8 years old so we would be able to properly defend ourselves. Needless to say, he did not raise us to be passive. He also was sure that we understood how to respect and honor authority by knowing when and where it is best to just keep your mouth shut.

I was a stubborn kid and there were many times I had to learn that lesson the hard way. Fortunately, by the time I enlisted in the Air Force I had learned the hard lessons which saved me lot of grief. It was clear that some of the guys I served with were never taught that lesson and had to learn how to keep their mouth shut the military way which rarely takes a caring parental approach to anything.

One of the best lessons my dad taught me as a kid was

how to face and overcome my fears. The care my dad took in raising me prepared me for life. I've always felt like he gave me a bag full of tools to carry with me to help on the journey. I can reach into the bag when needed and pull out a principle. One of the tools he always made sure I had in the bag is the Holy Bible. For that I am eternally grateful. I'm confident that <u>Success Motivation for Children</u> will help you prepare the same bag of tools for your sons and daughters and provide you with a renewed perspective on life.

Rob Teel

Acknowledgements

Thanks to God who created me, loves me, and gave me the ideas for this book.

Thanks to my wife who has ever believed in me and passionately supported me during the writing of this work.

Thanks to Nina Caputo for the cover of this book.

My sister Linda labored tirelessly editing, giving suggestions, and emailing back and forth in preparing the manuscript. Thanks a million to one of the sweetest sisters in the world!

Finally, I want to thank my family, piano students, parishioners, friends, and colleagues who provided such a rich backdrop of experiences for explaining my ideas, without which, this would not have been possible.

CHAPTER 1

Where does success motivation come from?

The original idea of success comes from the Bible.

God spoke to Joshua and said: "Do not let this Book of the Law depart from your mouth; meditate on it day and night, so that you may be careful to do everything written in it. Then you will be prosperous and *successful*." Joshua 1:8

Good advice for all of us!

You *will* be successful my friend if you meditate on the right words, speak the right words, and then act on the right words!

Joshua was Moses' assistant throughout the exodus of the Children of Israel from Egypt to Palestine in the 15th century B.C. He watched forty years as Moses brilliantly led the Jews out of captivity and into the land of promise. When Moses died, God gave the leadership of His people and conquest of Canaan to Joshua.

Joshua was a very successful leader because he learned to listen to Moses. He watched Moses as he struggled with leading the people and trying to hear from God.

Knowing how to be successful boils down to listening, observing, and following the right people, the right ideas, and the right values.

Knowing how to be successful boils down to listening, observing, and following the right people, the right ideas, and the right values.

Success is possible because the Bible - being the core of all sound principles concerning success - has been around and available to us for centuries.

Joshua is one of many examples of those who knew that the fundamental principles of success begin with finding and acting on the truth. The two most important realities we can get in touch with in our world is first, the truth about God and second, the truth about ourselves.

Serving in ministry and teaching piano for many years has afforded me the opportunity to observe kids in all kinds of settings. Through these experiences, I've come to realize that kids are motivated by simple things - like adults being kind to them - or like compliments and positive feedback. Once you realize what motivates kids, it's not hard to influence them in a positive way.

It's not hard to show kids you care. It just takes a little unselfishness, a little getting out of your self, looking at them and observing what matters to them.

I'm not going to say it's easy to *take the time* to be interested in their world. They are little people and just as they get bored with our grown up world, adults can get easily bored with theirs. I can barely keep up with my grandsons playing x-box 360 games or any other video games that seem to occupy them 24/7. I don't have time to get acquainted with the games they spend every waking moment playing so here's what I tell them: "I and most grown-ups have very busy schedules and rarely have time to practice the games you're playing. That's why you're always beating me!" I try to connect with them in other ways, such as helping them with a school project, playing football, or just hanging out and talking to them. I encourage them to find other things to do besides stare at a game all day, headphones on, controller in hand, mesmerized, and barely able to speak.

All humans need recognition. All of us crave significance and a safe place of acceptance. Many kids today are missing these most basic and critical components needed to be confident and successful. The profound tragedy is this: ***the needed ingredients for success could so easily be provided if only the adults around kids would open their eyes and ears to their needs.*** Adults are often caught up in criticizing kids instead.

Let me ask you a question.

What would your reaction be if one of your kids fell off the couch and split his head open? Would you say, "Daddy and Mommy told you not to do that - but did you listen? Nooo. When are you going to start minding? We can't believe you did that since we just told you not to." What's it going to take to convince you? Were you even listening?"

I don't think you would do that. You would run to scoop him up in your arms and make sure he's ok. Your first reaction would be hugging, loving, comforting, and checking the wound, making sure he didn't need stitches. You would wet a towel and clean the injury and comfort his crying. You would speak words reassuring him that everything is going to be o.k. You would tell him that daddy and mommy love him.

Granted, emergencies don't happen like that everyday but when kids are in the picture, minor catastrophes seem to crop up on a daily basis. How different might the outcome of those minor problems be if parents changed their focus. Instead of fixating on children's bad behavior, why not take positive steps to gently correct them or explain the importance of developing their listening skills?

If your child falls off the couch, perhaps later when he's ok and not crying, you might talk to him about being more careful and to heed

Success motivation begins with self value. It begins when kids and all human beings find out who they are.

warnings and listen. You may explain that bad choices and wrong actions produce hurtful consequences.

Everyday parents have opportunities to lead. If they look for opportunities and embrace them as opportunities - not obstacles or inconveniences - many great teaching moments will open up that have the potential of deeply touching kids with wisdom and compassion.

Almost absent from American culture today is the passing on of solid values to the next generation. There's a growing list of kids who literally 'go missing' in our nation every year - missing parents, missing direction, missing values, and missing self worth.

Kids today are facing incredible challenges. Pernicious, captivating, and life-absorbing problems are overtaking them like a tsunami. One of the most profound ways grown-ups contribute to the challenges kids face is by simply ignoring them. Letting kids fend for themselves, emotionally, relationally, and spiritually, is not a good idea.

Child neglect and abuse is at an all time high and is leaving an awful stain on our nation's conscience. Many kids today are being raised as if they're strangers, or worse, as if they're a bother, a nuisance, or an unwanted distraction. Many parents today are caught up with everything ***but*** parenting. Given the growing tide of physical abuse in the home and the increase of grandparents raising their grandchildren, it has become apparent that many parents are lost in their own world, simply too preoccupied with themselves to notice their kids. I hope teaching 'success motivation' will radically change that trend.

Where does 'success motivation' begin?

Success motivation begins with ***self value.*** It begins when kids and all human beings find out who they are.

Contemporary psychology teaches that self value comes from succeeding.

I don't think so. Succeeding builds confidence and produces a good feeling about your self but it does not produce self value. It's difficult to move forward in life without some "wins" under your belt, but "winning" falls short. I think everyone is born into this world to win. To truly win, however, you must find out who you are first.

Success for kids begins when they learn how to deal with failure. Let me ask you a question: "If adults have a bad feeling about failing, how much worse do you think children feel when they fail?" It's natural for a child or teenager to conclude that ***they are what they do.*** In other words – they ***are dumb*** when they act dumb, they ***are*** *incompetent* when they make mistakes, and they ***are*** *weak* when they fail. I don't know about you but I hate failing and it only makes it worse if someone rubs my nose in it.

Children tend to swallow the negative stuff of their lives hook, line, and sinker. The negative stuff about them may not be true but they totally accept it as reality. Children are inclined to internalize everything, especially the negative. They're not able to differentiate between the negative around them and the negative inside them. Kids live in an imperfect world like the rest of us but they can't tell the difference between what **others** do to defeat them and what **they** do to defeat themselves. That's why it's so critical for adults in their lives to be gracious and patient with kid's mess ups.

It's critical to speak identity into their lives. It's important to see into their future and not focus so much on the here and now. Kids will make it through if parents will support them even when they're foolish. Let's never say foolishness is alright but let's always say our kids are alright!

When I was in my mid teens my dad and mom took me and my friend Jon on a camping trip. The first order of the day was to open the trailer-tent and set it up for the night. I eagerly tackled the job but quickly ran into complications. I didn't understand how to open it and stood their scratching my head.

My dad didn't notice my hesitation at first but after a few minutes he walked over to assess the progress. When he saw I was in over my head he said, "Let's get someone over here with brains to set up this tent," implying I had no brains but my friend Jon did.

That hurt more than words can express but I buried it. I denied the pain it caused me. In my head I immediately started my own private conversation, "Wow, my dad is right. I'm not very smart. Why couldn't I figure that out? I'm intellectually inferior to Jon and therefore less of a person. What kind of flunky am I?"

That failure made me feel totally dejected and being compared to my friend made me want to die. At the time I didn't have any defense mechanisms working - that might have helped. When my dad compared me to my friend, I swallowed it 100%. I accepted it completely as 'the truth.' I didn't have a brain like Jon. I was a loser.

I questioned my dad's love for me because I was dumb. That was depressing.

Failure makes you feel bad. Success makes you feel better. Since a good performance always seemed to help get me out of the pit of despair, after the camping event I thought the answer to my problems was to get smarter. I tried harder in school. I tried to think more clearly. Surely I would feel better if I were just a bit brighter, a little more informed, a little more prepared. Trying harder and pursuing higher education later would solve everything, right? Reflecting on this now, I realize this camping experience was only the beginning of a path that led me deeper and deeper into pain and disappointment.

Succeeding instead of failing is a good thing - but it's not the answer to a better self esteem. The truth is, our self esteem does not come from succeeding or from a good performance. Let me explain because understanding self esteem is at the core of success motivation.

Though success may help ease one's feelings of low self worth, success can't permanently remove those feelings. As a matter of fact, success may embed those feelings deeper.

Success is transient. It comes and goes as does failure. That's the nature of success and failure. ***Believing you're of worth in spite of success or failure is the key to breaking free.***

Succeeding comes from self esteem, not self esteem from succeeding. Being successful is not the basis of who we are. Neither is it the basis of who a child is. The heart of who you are is a gift. It doesn't begin with being good at something. It doesn't come from earning it, deserving it, or living up to it. Discovering this truth is like finding the answer that unlocks everything else in life.

The old adage goes, "What comes first, the chicken or the egg?" Does belief in your self produce success or does success produce belief in your self? Good news! Success motivation begins when you accept yourself as an imperfect yet lovable person worthy of forgiveness.

Success follows self value, self value doesn't follow success.

Think about that.

If your self esteem depends on success, then failure means you're worthless. The problem with this thinking is the inevitability of your own personal failure. With no self esteem as a result of failure, you're disqualified to be accepted. Failure classifies you as a reject. It separates you from all the important and commendable people in life. Failure equals your unimportance. But it's not true! Let me ask you this: "Who has never failed?" No one! How do people then overcome their failure? By discovering success and failure don't determine self worth.

If you believe that your failure defines who you are and predicts what you will be, then you are going to be in a world of hurt the rest of your life. The internal belief that 'if I fail I'm worth nothing' is a very powerful negative motivator! It's a real downer!

On the other hand, if you believe self esteem comes from your Creator bestowed upon you as a bequest, failure doesn't matter. It doesn't determine who you are and what you're going to be. God has made you and accepted you in spite of your failure. You are free to fail without losing who you are and free to succeed without going on a massive ego trip. You're free to succeed because the pressure is gone from trying to somehow earn your worth or value. No one can achieve any lasting success without believing in themselves but no one can believe in themselves unless they believe in something bigger than themselves.

Success motivation begins when you seek and accept forgiveness for your failure. It begins when you start believing in yourself. It begins the moment you believe ***you are*** the person God made and loves. Success doesn't come from any where else. Kid's are very vulnerable and need to hear this message from the significant others in their lives. They need this message demonstrated through a loving parent who affirms them constantly. They don't need to be listening to the other negative messages life is sending them or listening to their own disapproving dialogues going on in their heads about what they aren't or who they can't be.

You can't put a price tag on a child's self worth or on your own. It's an endowment from God, period. You can't earn it, perform for it, be smart enough for it, rich enough for it, or rightly positioned to receive it. You inherit self esteem because you are a child of God, born into this world with nothing but "gifts." Your arms, legs, face, and brain are all gifts! You didn't even need to think about it, it just happened!

Maybe you were planned and maybe you weren't. It doesn't matter. You are worthy and lovely simply because you are. God made you in His image and designed you to know Him. That's your value. It's impossible to try and change that fact by 'making it,' succeeding, or winning, or by pointing to some important event in your life as proof of your worth. These truths are absolutely critical for kids to awaken to if they want to succeed!

Without this awareness, it's highly likely that kids will suffer for the rest of their lives. They will keep running around looking for approval in all the wrong places and doing anything to get it.

I used to suffer from severe performance anxiety. More often than not whenever I played the piano in public, I would choke. It didn't matter if I practiced, memorized, rehearsed, or how well I "knew" the piece. When I started playing, my hands would begin to shake, my heart would begin to pound like thunder, then my mind would begin racing like a Nascar dragster. The result: a performance disaster!

I've asked myself over and over again why I did this to myself. **It was a defect in my belief system!** I've agonized over this and tried to get in touch with my true feelings and finally realized I was accepting this fallacy: no matter how well I perform, it will never be good enough. Talk about self defeating! That sabotaged my self confidence and put me in checkmate every time!

I've come a long way in overcoming performance anxiety because I've learned to accept myself in spite of my foibles and imperfections. When I've inquired of concert pianists, college professors, and other performers how they've overcome the pressure of performing, I learned they too experienced performance anxiety! Discovering that helped me to relax, listen to my music, and enjoy what I was doing.

Kids grab hold of success when they grab hold of who they are: created in God's image with inestimable value. Kids who get this early in their development will be acquainted with happiness, enjoy themselves, and grow into healthy individuals.

Parents have a huge influence on instilling this faith in their children and it's imparted to a huge degree by **how** parents treat their kids.

Does embracing this premise mean not correcting them? Does it mean kids aren't a royal pain sometimes? Does it mean they don't make mistakes and annoy us? No.

The difference is beginning at a new place of understanding.

Often parents think that self worth is equivalent to a child's good behavior. That belief frequently leads them to superimpose unbalanced discipline without the other half of the equation - unconditional love.

Trying to control a child's behavior simply through putting greater and greater pressure on them backfires! Instilling values I think is a better approach. Touching them with love and acceptance makes it easier for them to receive boundaries. Trying to force them brings everything to a grinding halt. Someone once said, R+R-R=R. Rules + regulations – relationship = rebellion.

Kids grow up in one of two ways: with coping tools, skills for handling criticism, and healthy ways of looking at themselves, or they grow up with negative input and wrong messages about who they are and therefore develop no coping tools or skills for handling criticism or healthy ways of seeing themselves. They launch out in life off balance and twisting their ankle every time they take a step. They grow up fighting with themselves and everyone else. They quarrel with their parents, teachers, friends, and law enforcement. Why? Nobody told them they were acceptable. Nobody told them they were loveable and truly acted that out toward them in a meaningful way.

Success Motivation for Kids

What happens when kids fail to receive the message that they are of worth purely because they are made in God's image? Without this simple fundamental message: 'you are loved,' 'you are accepted,' 'you are of worth just because you are,' no amount of extra 'convincing' later on in life may compensate for it. Good coping skills will be nonexistent and kids won't be able to accept constructive criticism. They'll literally be left without the ability to get along with others. This unhealthy reality prevents them from making good decisions regarding a host of important issues in their lives. Kids will make huge messes for themselves and all the people around them if they don't acquire this. Developing a realistic, strong, and stable sense of self worth then, is urgent.

There is a vast chasm between those who believe in self worth as a matter of trying harder or being smarter, and those who believe our maker bestows self worth upon us. This is kind of an ideological dividing line in psychology. There are different schools of thought about how children develop into healthy individuals and these philosophies profoundly influence how we raise kids. We need to concentrate on building relationship with our children and building their sense of self acceptance.

If we focus on the outward by making kids work harder, study more, discipline themselves, and teaching them to "pull themselves together," It sounds good but doesn't deliver unless we preface it by accepting and valuing them first.

Recognizing that personal significance is gifted to us is critical. Only then can we focus on the outward by

Recognizing that personal significance is gifted to us is critical.

helping kids apply themselves, work harder, and improve. Accepting and loving kids and teaching them to love themselves just because *they are* is the beginning of success motivation.

THE 1ST KEY TO SUCCESS MOTIVATION:

Lead children into unconditionally accepting themselves.

CHAPTER 2

Parent's critical role in building children's self worth

> *Attempting to control behavior by imposing pressure instead of discipline hardens the heart.*

If children are going to be truly motivated, they must be given the opportunity to fail. ***How*** parents handle failure is critical. Children need opportunities to make choices and face the consequences, good or bad, but instead of ridiculing, criticizing, or over-reacting, parents need to change the focus. "O.K., you are going to be disciplined for what you did, but more importantly, let's talk about how you can make better decisions in the future."

Kids should be respected enough to make age appropriate decisions on their own, like what color shirt they prefer to wear. There are many decisions we can all make which have no moral implications, they're just a matter of taste. So give your kids lots of those kinds of choices to begin with.

Attempting to control behavior by imposing pressure instead of discipline hardens the heart. It meets with resistance. It meets with resentment. Why? Pressure strips

Children need to find a basis on which to believe in themselves.

children of getting in touch with their preferences, the chance to make choices, and to face the consequences good or bad.

Discipline is not pressure. It's following through on giving consequences when somebody didn't listen or do what they were told. Parental pressure - in contrast to discipline - comes in the form of verbal threats and nagging. Effective discipline is clear cut. You've shared your expectations, you've explained the consequences for breaking the rules, now it's time to enforce the rules and let the kids live with the consequences.

My wife Debbie remembers her mom taking her shopping and asking questions like, "Do you like that blouse?" Debbie would say "yes," I like it very much." Then her mom would continue, "Well, you just think you like it, but I'm buying you this other one because you'll be glad someday you have this other one." Talk about confusing a kid! No wonder Debbie grew up not knowing what she wanted and feeling guilty when she got it!

Are kids really happier and better off when parents make decisions like that for them? No, kids are unhappier and worse off.

Something needs to happen to change the way children view themselves. They need to see themselves as important persons of dignity with a purpose and a destiny. If they are truly going to gain a sense of self worth, then they must know they're ok. One of the ways that happens is when they're allowed their preferences within reasonable limits.

Children need to find a basis on which to believe

in themselves. When they discover God believes in them, **nothing is impossible**. Kids will accept themselves when they discover how special they are. That happens in great degree through the adults in their lives who are close to them and interact with them everyday. Their family of origin in particular has a profound impact on the growth of their self value.

What do kids want and need most from the grown ups in their lives? They want and need affirmation, praise, value, and respect. Does that mean throwing out boundaries? Does that mean raising them without a set of rules? Of course not. They need wisdom and discretion. However, rules only serve to guide kids toward doing the right thing. Rules don't change them. They need an over riding sense of purpose to do that.

Have you ever known anyone who was truly successful in life who went around saying things like, "I'm no good, I'm a flake, I'm a failure, I can't do anything right?" Neither have I. People who are motivated don't say things like that. Yet I must admit this is where I've personally suffered through many valleys. No one told me when I was young that I had any control over what I was thinking. Many thoughts about my self growing up were unconstructive and harmful. The good news is, I decided years ago to embrace God's love for me and stop constantly criticizing myself. People like myself who have a healthy self concept have managed to dump negative baggage out of their lives and have stopped speaking death over themselves.

Unfortunately, all of us carry leftover 'stuff' from our childhood into adult life. The beginning of success is found in understanding our past and getting liberated from the negative aspects of it. I believe it's urgent today that parents understand especially while their own children are growing up, they alone have the greatest control over their development of self worth than anyone else in their world.

There is no one else on planet earth who influences a child's future

Parents by far have the greatest influence in setting low limits on their children or encouraging high limits.

through the development or the destruction of their self worth than parents. The input children receive from parents during their early years **sets their course for a life time!** I spoke recently to a young friend who was saved through my ministry. He never knew his real dad and his step father and mother were abusive. He continually struggles today with liking himself or seeing himself as successful. He finds it hard to keep a job and is very critical of himself. His home life most certainly impacted him and contributed to the handicap of not believing in him self. I told him one day after we talked about his dilemma that he would probably be facing this challenge for the rest of his life. It could have been so different if his dad had been there for him. The good news is he's changing one day at a time.

Parents by far have **the greatest** influence in setting low limits on their children or encouraging high limits. They hold the key to building or destroying confidence and it doesn't take much to shake a child's confidence.

Much time and effort is required to build confidence in a child and only moments to obliterate it. The needed groundwork for taking the limits off of kids begins with statements and actions they hear and observe from the significant others in their lives everyday. Positive words, encouraging, accepting tones, someone listening to their ideas and caring about their hurts are the building blocks of self worth. The statements and actions directed toward kids in common situations are the greatest teachers which influence their thinking and opinions of themselves.

Children are very good at picking up on the most

subtle forms of rejection. They don't fully understand it, but somehow they can feel it. They can hear the voice inflection, they can see the body language, they can see the disapproving look. They understand when a storm is brewing and about to break out on them.

One day a few years ago, I was giving piano lessons to two brothers in their home. I'm not using their real names but Jim was about 11 years old and was sitting at the piano with me at his side. Jason the younger brother walked in to say "hello" and give his brother a hug. We were talking and laughing and enjoying a brief moment of fun when the mother marched into the room and shouted at Jason, "What do you think you're doing in here?"

I looked up at Jason who by this time was doing a Michael Jackson moonwalk backwards. A look of terror had come over his face. He ran into the other room not to be seen again until it was his turn to take a piano lesson.

Jason's mother Joan had often complained that Jason was "jumpy" and could not focus. He was not making great progress on the piano and would fume whenever he made a mistake. His face would turn red when he missed a note and he would pound the keys in frustration. His mother was constantly interjecting her 'discipline' to keep him in 'order.' She would yell, criticize, and point out everything he was doing wrong and picking on every move he made.

To make matters worse, when Jason would make a mistake on the piano, his mother and brother would laugh and his mom would encourage the older brother to criticize him.

One day after an unsuccessful attempt to change his behavior by yelling, Jason's mother noticed that the lesson went well anyway, in spite of her failed attempts to gain control over his "unruly" behavior. After the lesson that day she asked me privately if I needed her help in getting Jason to pay attention. I assured her that if I needed her I would certainly ask for her help.

Jason's mom stopped interfering and things slowly changed for the better. Jason stopped throwing tantrums and cursing under his breath and abusing the piano keys. He began making progress.

I have no doubt in my mind that Jason's mother loved him. I have no doubt in my mind that she wanted the very best for both her boys. Yet everyday, she was "shouting" a different message. I'm sure she thought she was doing the right thing but she was actually doing the opposite.

How could Jason's mom think she was doing one thing but in reality be doing just the opposite?

That's a big question. For the moment, allow me to interpret what I think Jason heard his mother say when she came in the room with elevated voice and contorted facial expressions? I think Jason heard: "I'm an idiot. I'm a loser. I'm no good. I'm not wanted." Did his mom know she communicated that? I don't think so.

What may have been Jason's feelings? I don't think Jason could get fully in touch with his true feelings at that point in his life nor could he consciously process what was happening other than feeling abject fear and anger. What feelings do you think you would have? I believe within Jason's heart, the implications of his mother's actions were beginning to formulate a vivid image - yet not distinguishable enough to express verbally at that moment, but nonetheless intense – "I'm a reject!"

Jason and his mom I'm sure weren't aware of it then, but both Jason and his mother are almost certain to pay dearly for his mother's actions, especially if she continues to move in this direction with him. Both she and her son will pay, now and later.

Jason will pay now by continuing to be jumpy, unfocused, and frustrated with himself whenever he makes a mistake. His mother's "not so subtle" message of intolerance will continue to evoke an unfavorable response from him, which will almost certainly grow into Jason rejecting himself and rebelling against her.

His anger - which he's burying now - will invariably turn into resentment and outward rebellion later on. Bitterness will no doubt go deeper and drive a wedge between he and his mother.

If Jason's mom does not change her approach, she will continue to be frustrated with Jason's lack of concentration and self control. She will most likely forge ahead more forcibly and become more and more determined to control Jason's behavior as he continues to resist more and more her efforts to change him. Her unproductive approach of controlling him will fuel her frustration and Jason will probably act in increasingly uncooperative ways causing him to exasperate her even more. She will pay later by having a teenager on her hands acting out his hurt and rejection on everyone around him. He will become her worst nightmare.

Sound familiar?

What could Jason's mom have done differently and more effectively?

Joan could have appreciated that Jason is a social kid. She could have joined in with the fun of talking. She could have been grateful that Jason loves his brother. She could have made positive comments about Jason's interest in music but remind him it's not his turn yet.

By the way, when it was the older brother's turn for a lesson next time, I planned in advance to make a point. When he made a mistake in his lesson, I reached over and held his hand on the mistake and with a slightly elevated voice said, "You made a mistake!" He responded with a fearful low voice, "I know, I know," then he began fidgeting uncomfortably. I said, "Don't worry about the mistake." "If you don't make mistakes it means you're not learning anything." So I let go

> *There are a thousand subtle ways in which worth or rejection is communicated verbally and nonverbally.*

of his hand and said, "Would you do me a favor?" He said, "Sure, anything!" "Next time your brother makes a mistake, don't make fun of him alright?" He said, "Alright, I won't."

I noticed that Jason's older brother never made fun of his little brother in front of me again. His mother backed off and things got better. A really harmful pattern that was damaging Jason slowly began to change.

Self esteem isn't something kids learn in a classroom or even in a deliberate teaching setting at home. Self esteem is profoundly influenced by the way they're talked to and treated day in and day out.

Many parents need a loud wake-up call regarding this.

You don't have to be a genius to figure out when you're not wanted. Kids are very sensitive to being put off, even if it looks like they're handling it just fine in the present. Believe me, a time-bomb is ticking.

Parents don't have to ring a bell and hold a class session to teach their children self worth. Everyday, every hour, in every situation, parents are either adding worth to their kids or subtracting worth, and it's all in **how** they speak to them and **how** they treat them.

There are a thousand subtle ways in which worth or rejection is communicated verbally and nonverbally.

We're all familiar with the obvious negative messages - rolling the eyes, hands on the hips, tapping of the foot, shaking the index finger in a kid's face. There are also other more subtle forms of rejection such as questions parents ask kids that don't have real answers like, "Why don't you practice like you're brother?" or "Why did you do that?" or "What is your problem?" Always intervening in a kid's thought processes and giving them the answer before they can think about it is another form of rejection. The message that implies is: "What kind of moron are you that you need me to constantly give you the answers to everything?"

Why don't adults leave well enough alone? Why can't they take their controlling hands off of God's gifts to them? Some parents think that backing off of controlling their kids would lead to embarrassing them. Other parents feel their discipline is "the only right way." Still others may fear that if they don't control every move their child makes, their child will turn out bad.

To gain control, you must lose it. Yes, that's right. You still make the rules, the big difference is the way you handle broken rules. Do you attack? Do you say nasty and unloving things? Call names? Suggest a child is stupid?

Love is expressed in loving words, a kind touch, and a listening ear. It's expressed in giving your child respect, teaching them that it's o.k. to make a mistake, teaching them it's o.k. to talk to you about what they feel is unfair. It's also amazingly liberating to give your kids permission to tell you what they think you're doing wrong. It's also amazingly humbling! They will keep you on your toes, believe me, but it will release a channel of communication that nothing else could ever open.

Negative and unprofitable verbal forms of rejection are too common in homes today. Yelling, name calling, impatience with everything a kid does, threatening, and demeaning a child's capabilities happens too often. How many know that kind of treatment does not create an atmosphere of acceptance, tolerance, or lead to change?

Wouldn't you agree that positive messages like praise, patience, and personally identifying with a child's failure and letting them know you have been guilty of the very same thing is incredibly productive and life-changing?!

Unfortunately, many parents - and consequently children - are not acquainted with positive messages like praise, a caring touch and quality time. The language of love is not spoken in their home. Instead, parents are in the habit of fault finding, blowing their top, impatiently criticizing, and not taking time to listen.

There are many other ways rejection is acted out toward kids. For instance, when parents don't allow children enough freedom corresponding to their age, that is a form of rejection.

Carol was from a devout Christian home. Her parents refused to let her go out alone with her friends. They were there right after school to pick her up. She was not allowed to socialize to any great degree unless her friends came to her house. When she was 13, the pastor's son of the church they attended invited her to go miniature golfing. No way. She was not allowed. As the years passed I noticed a great deal of anger, resentment, and bitterness in this girl. The moment she turned 18 she moved in with her boyfriend. She rejected all of the good values her parents tried to give her.

Could there have been a better way? Absolutely! Restricting this girl from the outside world was an abysmal failure. It produced the opposite outcome her parents were looking for. It was a form of rejection. I knew her parents. I know they loved her. They just didn't know **how** to love her. They didn't know how to let go.

Not listening to children's feelings but instead over-riding them with a statement like, "Oh, don't worry about that, it's no big deal," is another form of rejection. Not allowing kids to fail is another one.

When I was about 10 years old, I would come in from my day to the family dinner table and desperately want to talk about the important things that had happened to me that day. I wouldn't get two words out of my mouth before my Dad stopped me to correct my grammar. At that point, I became tongue tied, nervous, and I was not able to finish.

It took me years to get in touch with my true feelings about those times of frustration and the wounds I suffered at the hand of my well-intentioned father.

At the time I thought, "My dad is right, I can't talk right. I really need to work on speaking correctly. I shouldn't even open my mouth if I can't talk right. I'm stupid." I grew up stuffing those and other feelings down so deep inside that it effectively prevented me from knowing my true feelings about super important issues in my life and wondering why I struggled with depression.

Without my dad's awareness I'm sure, each time he corrected me and didn't let me finish speaking, the unintended, hidden, but very hurtful message was: "Your feelings aren't important, speaking correctly is!" It has taken years and lots of practice for me to get in touch with my true feelings about significant issues in my life and communicate those feelings without fear.

There were many years of my young life that I was depressed without knowing what to call it. I didn't recognize the source of my depression until I was in the middle of reading a book one day. I came to a place in the book where the author asked me to picture my father sitting in front of me. "What would you say to your father if he were right in front of you?" The author mused.

As I pictured my dad in front of me, I began feeling very angry and deeply hurt. "Why didn't you let me talk?" I said out loud. "Why wasn't what I wanted to say important?" I broke into tears. I don't think I could have ever managed to get in touch with those feelings while my father was still living. It had been a while since he had passed away. I was free to feel now. There was no more fear. My Dad had no idea what injury he had caused.

Very rarely have I run into parents who actually say they don't love their children. Almost all parents say they love their children and I think they mean it! Yet, **<u>how</u>** they love their children is different. Many parents are completely unaware of what they're really communicating to their kids.

What you say and ***how*** you say it is how children will interpret their life and how they will interact with others. There is no other way. To motivate children, they have to be ***loved with words and actions and treated with dignity***.

> *To motivate children, they have to be loved with words and actions and treated with dignity.*

THE 2nd KEY TO SUCCESS MOTIVATION:

Impart self value to kids with words, actions, and affection.

CHAPTER 3

"SELF ESTEEM" – PSYCHCOBABBLE OR GOSPEL?

> *What we know and believe about ourselves directly impacts the way we relate to the world around us.*

Numerous psychology textbooks used in universities today suggest that if persons can just manage to get enough 'wins' under their belt, create enough positive experiences, and receive enough positive input from others - they will arrive at self esteem. This popular notion has been around for a long time.

On a certain level, success does build confidence and confidence seems to endow self-value. Yet, as I stated in chapter 1, self-esteem does not come from success or any other external source.

What we know and believe about ourselves directly impacts the way we relate to the world around us. It also affects the way we treat the kids in our lives thereby influencing the way they respond to their world.

Our first parents stepped into a major identity crises when Eve believed the lie that she was "not enough." Like us, Adam and Eve were created in the image of God. Eve *was* enough. She was lovable and capable. Adam was created innocent and good, adequate to fulfill his every dream.

There were two trees in the garden, the tree of life, and the tree of the knowledge of good and evil. The Lord told Adam and Eve to stay away from the tree of knowledge.

"Now the serpent was more crafty than any of the wild animals the Lord God had made. He said to the woman, "Did God really say, "You must not eat from any tree in the garden? The woman said to the serpent, "We may eat fruit from the trees in the garden, but God did say, "You must not eat fruit from the tree that is in the middle of the garden, and you must not touch it, or you will die." "You will not surely die," the serpent said to the woman. "For God knows that when you eat of it your eyes will be opened, and you will be like God, knowing good and evil." When the woman saw that the fruit of the tree was good for food and pleasing to the eye, and also desirable for gaining wisdom, she took some and ate it. She also gave some to her husband, who was with her, and he ate it." (Genesis 3:1-6)

Eve allowed herself to be convinced to eat from the tree of knowledge because the serpent lied to her about who she was. At the end of their conversation, she believed she would become 'greater' than she already was so she bit into the fruit. She gave the fruit to Adam to "help" him see his greater potential. Instead of helping of course, it caused them to fall, and the entire human race fell with them.

Let's look a little closer at what really happened. Eve was easily deceived apparently because she had a low view of herself. Adam went along with Eve because he did not

---

Instead of bringing freedom, enlightenment, and success, taking the fruit brought on a greater sense of failure.

want to lose her. The serpent was successful in beguiling Eve into the delusion that God's way of fashioning her was inferior to what she could have been. Eve believed the lie that God was withholding something good from her and Adam.

William James, the father of modern psychology said, "There is a restiveness in man, an inherent sense of failure." I think Eve got in touch with the "restiveness" inside her and gave vent to it. Instead of bringing freedom, enlightenment, and success, taking the fruit brought on a greater sense of failure. She turned her back on the truth, believed a lie, and disobeyed God. "For all have sinned and fall short of the glory of God." (Romans 3:23)

Eve was not satisfied with what was: her innocence in a perfect environment with an innocent husband, loved by God and living in paradise. God would come out and talk with them in the cool of the evening. They didn't really have any hard work to do. They were living a wonderful life of peace. They had it all. It didn't rain on the earth at the time because subterranean springs watered the ground. Adam and Eve didn't even have any storms or inclement weather to deal with!

Yet, they gave it all up to chase an illusion. They gave up the best for the worst. Why does this sound so familiar? Why does this so resemble us? We gain money, possessions, and fame, only to be dissatisfied with them. We achieve success, good health, a clear mind, and good relationships but we want more. We obtain educational degrees, positions of status, and material possessions, but burn with lust, hatred, anger, bitterness, or regret. Someone once stated, "When it's hot, man wants it cold, when it's cold, man wants it hot. As a general rule, man wants what is not." That's us isn't it?

Adam and Eve were both already of incalculable value. They had already been approved of God. They were already the crowning jewels of God's creation. They already lived in an unpolluted, unspoiled, and incredible environment. They didn't live in the slums of New York City. They had never experienced poverty or government taxation or oppression. There was no crime and no criminals. There was nothing to fear and nothing to dread. Yet, they were convinced - with the help of the adversary - that they were missing something. They were convinced to throw everything away on a whim. They ate the forbidden fruit with the misguided hope of becoming *more* than they were.

Theologically speaking, the consequence of the devil's lie caused Adam and Eve to lose their relationship with God, hide themselves in fear from the very one who loved them and could help them, and passed the sin on to the rest of us. When they lost their relationship with God through disobedience, instead of becoming "more," they became less and cut themselves off from the only real life and source of genuine value. Instead of becoming like God, their decision gave rise to destruction, war, and want.

Isn't that a description of all of us? We're all created in the image of God and yet we "eat" all kinds of evil fruit trying to find "more" significance than we already have. We'll give up anything to be more attractive, smarter, richer, or more important. The emptiness inside speaks to us of our deficiencies yet all our attempts to find worth and value end in finding more of everything but happiness. Like Adam and Eve, we find the tree of knowledge but not the tree of life. Kids are caught in the battle of 'not feeling enough' beginning at the earliest ages when they don't want to share their toys with Johnny. They cry, pout, complain, and fight when things don't go their way. Human nature is definitely a part of them from day one along with insecurities, fears, and uncertainty about who they are in the scope of this big wide world. We find more education, more wealth, more prestige, but not more life!"

We're already important! We're already significant and valuable! We don't need to do anything more to gain an advantage. There are all kinds of "fruit" this world promises that are suppose to lead us to greater satisfaction. However, like Adam and Eve in their search, we simply get more knowledge from the "fruit" not the truth. We desperately search for purpose and meaning not knowing we already have it.

People all over the world today are still buying into the lie spoken in the Garden of Eden – "I'm not enough." "I need props, people, support, recognition, achievement, money, or education to "be enough". Humans never seem to arrive at being content with themselves or their lot in life. America is carrying on a raging love affair with looking young, wanting to be rich and famous, wanting the dream, wanting it all, but never quite arriving at it.

How does this ingrown deficit affect the kids we're raising? Correct or incorrect, kids often determine their self-worth by what parents say and how they compare themselves to peers. This is how they calculate their self worth.

Like adults kids also feel "restive." Kids also search for significance. They also need recognition. William James also said, "The deepest principle in human nature is the craving to be appreciated." Without getting the true message that self-value is because **they are**, kids like all other generations before them, will fall into a pit of striving to be 'enough' and behaving in all kinds of unproductive and destructive ways to find "being enough." Just a passing observation of the culture of Hollywood reflects the quintessence of this truth. I've noticed when innocent talented individuals find "success" in Hollywood, it's not long before they are 'in over their

> *People all over the world today are still buying into the lie spoken in the Garden of Eden – "I'm not enough."*

> *Many who make it to the top remain restless, unfulfilled, and continue to search for just "one more of something" to find peace.*

heads,' caught in a power struggle for their souls. Many normal, fine people who get sucked into that world often begin acting in the most bizarre, unkind, hurtful, and insane ways. They get trapped into thinking they've arrived at the pinnacle.

Wins, successes, and the high opinions of others may help you feel better about yourself and depression can temporarily be helped by simply being productive. But even though being smart, clever, or strong may gain you a position or a job, it won't increase your self esteem. Perfect performance, more education, becoming a multi millionaire, or becoming better looking through some form of plastic surgery will also fail to deliver. Worth has already been granted.

My pride was inflated or deflated when I was growing up by the things I did. I thought, "If I could only get a better grade, hit the baseball farther, be cooler, smarter, more hip, more clever, then I would end up liking myself more because I then would be 'successful'." The "better feeling" about myself never materialized through outward success.

The more you achieve in life the more you want. If you become a doctor, you may conclude you're "just another doctor" among many others. If you become an attorney, your practice will take its place with thousands of other attorneys. If you become an actor, you're still not a superstar and that's just not enough, and on and on it goes. Many who make it to the top remain restless, unfulfilled, and continue to search for just "one more of something" to find peace. It reminds me of an old saying, "Happiness is not getting what you want, but wanting what you have."

The search for personal significance also exists within Christian ministry. I became an ordained minister years ago and was involved in full time ministry for decades. I loved serving in the ministry and responding to God's call on my life, yet I struggled with a low self esteem and a gnawing sense of failure. You would think a person called into the ministry would be free of this. I understood that God loved me, that I was accepted of Him and that my sins were forgiven, but I never thought any of my achievements were enough. I have since learned like the apostle Paul to say, "I care very little if I am judged by you or by any human court; indeed, I do not even judge myself." (I Corinthians 4:3)

When I was in my twenties, instead of being satisfied with what God had given me to do in the various positions I held, I would look at other youth ministries bigger and more successful and feel inferior and sub-par. I was continually striving to improve so that I could "become successful like the other guy." Dr. James Dobson was right when he said, "Comparison to others is destructive to a person's sense of self worth." I know that from first-hand experience!

I have always tried to remain humble with my achievements because I knew deep inside that my success came from God and it wouldn't be right to take the credit. But that didn't stop me from always wanting a bigger and bigger youth group and never being satisfied with what I had, even though I was doing my best.

My attitude didn't improve much when I became a pastor. I looked around and saw that there were other larger and more influential ministries than my own. My hopes of feeling better about myself because I was now a pastor, led to feeling worse because I could never achieve the greater and greater success I thought I needed to be important.

In reality, my success caused anxiety and unrest, not self esteem. My success drove me to want something larger and larger.

It took a process of time, a lot of soul searching, and God's help to jar me away from the hold "the race for success" had on me. I had to make a conscious choice to focus on what God had called me to do, not how well-known I would become by doing it. I needed to just love people and not worry about the rest. Mother Theresa said, "God does not require me to succeed, He only requires that I try."

Paul the apostle's voice now echoes in my mind reminding me how I am to walk on earth: "Therefore judge nothing before the appointed time; wait till the Lord comes. He will bring to light what is hidden in darkness and will expose the motives of men's hearts. At that time each will receive his praise from God." (I Corinthians 4:5)

I also faced the same sort of challenge with public speaking. I wanted to hit a grand slam every time I got up to speak. I wanted people to like me. I wanted to do a good job but my focus on the delivery interfered with saying it! To overcome this, I had to let go of trying to make everything sound like Billy Grahm and just say what I was given without worrying about what it sounded like!

We're taught in our culture in a thousand ways if we perform well, work harder, stick to the job, don't give up, study more, and strive for excellence, we'll achieve what others only wished they had - a greater sense of self value.

THAT'S A LIE!

We're told in school we need only to study and apply ourselves so that someday we'll be hired on a job making lots of money and live happily ever after. We're convinced that education is the answer to everything so education becomes the shrine at which our egos are burnished, our personalities galvanized, our futures secured! We're taught education is the key to success because it qualifies us more than someone else. Our culture bows down to the P.H.D. and universities given reverence because they're places where 'people find success.'

I'm not minimizing establishing a career and making a living as important achievements. Gaining an education is an essential tool for moving forward. However, these things have never provided the answer to any of man's inner emptiness.

Let's look at this from another viewpoint. Let's suppose for a moment that self esteem does come from our performance. Let's assume that self value *is* derived from education, acquired possessions, and our achievements. When you dig a little deeper into this thinking you find the **MOTHER OF ALL PREJUDICE, BIGOTRY, AND INTOLERANCE!**

Let me repeat that. The notion that one's personal worth is derived from achievement, I.Q., bank account, notoriety, etc., etc., etc., **IS THE ROOT OF ALL PREJUDICE, DISCRIMNATION, AND PRIDE ON PLANET EARTH!**

I realize that's a strong statement so let me explain.

If self worth originates from what I've earned, achieved, or performed, then **the greater my achievement, the greater my worth!**

Don't get me wrong, achievement is important. As a matter of fact, if you don't achieve, you're probably doing something very wrong. You'll end up on the street if you do nothing. Achievement has its place. It gives us personal fulfillment for the need to make progress. It's basic to man's survival. It pays our bills.

However, if success determines personal worth, then all those who haven't achieved as much as I have, are worth *less* than I am. All those who have achieved more, are worth *more*. Please think that through. We would never admit it out loud, but this notion is alive and thriving in most, if not all of us. Whole races, clans, and peoples have been judged wrongly by this worldly mindset and false standard.

> *The belief that achievement determines personal value is a sacred cultural ideology.*

Let's suppose a person decides to study hard and become a doctor. Based on the premise that self-worth comes from achievement - the doctor's personal significance will increase and he will be greater than those who did not study as hard or were not quite as intelligent. Since self worth becomes based on activity outside our selves, then achievement determines personal value. Anyone else less educated, less decorated, or less financially well-situated than ourselves, is then worth less than us!

The belief that achievement determines personal value is a sacred cultural ideology. Be honest. It's not likely you would ever admit it to anyone - but don't you think others who have worked harder, earned more money, managed to garner importance through their influence have achieved more worth? Our culture's value system blares this in deafening tones everywhere without a word being spoken and the volume is ever-increasing!

Whoever attains is a winner. Whoever is successful is "in." Whoever is smarter is preferred. You are a 'dummy' if you didn't make it. You're a loser if you've had some set backs. You're a reject compared to the rest of us if you struggle. The idea that my achievement equals my value, inevitably leads to the conclusion that those who do not achieve as much as I do, are worth less than I am. I am more, they are less.

If you subscribe to the philosophy that your self-value is based on what you've done, what you have gained, or the name you've made for yourself, then those around you who have not achieved to your level are inferior to you. You know deep inside it's not true. However, even if that belief system is only subconscious it makes you better than those who don't achieve as much, and less than those who have achieved more.

I suppose for many the idea that their self worth is not a result of their personal striving is a shock or like a slap in the face. Please don't take it as an insult. Every one of us has great value.

There is a prevalent belief system in psychology today that has been dubbed, "the just world philosophy." Boiled down, this philosophy espouses that good things happen to good people, and bad things happen to bad people. This is a deeply flawed concept, yet it hangs on in our society with incredible persistence. You might not want to own up to it, even to yourself, but what is your initial reaction to a bag lady on the street? Is she bad, negligent, undisciplined?

My reaction to bag persons in the past went something like this: "I feel sorry for them, yet the reason for their trouble is due to their own poor decisions or unwillingness to work, or because they're lazy or just plain losers. Their condition is a result of cause and effect. Their problems are the consequences of their own behavior." This kind of reasoning was usually enough to stop me from helping them.

You may think when you see someone at the bottom of the barrel, "they've probably been helped before and squandered what they were given." "They can't be trusted. *I'm* not on the street, so they don't have to be there either." And the scenarios could go on and on. Basically, we're all stuck in the belief system without even knowing it.

We judge others in comparison to ourselves. We judge others based on the belief that good things happen to good people and bad things happen to bad people.

To further illustrate this ask yourself, why in our culture are infants and toddlers given value, regardless of race, gender, status, or name? Children are small and weak, and largely ignorant of the world. They are innocent and haven't achieved anything of significance and yet we love and dote on them. Why?

There's a Bible personality who's experience flies in the face of the 'just world philosophy.' Job. The Bible describes Job as a righteous man, one who avoided evil. He lived a holy life before God and was a 'good person.' Yet, Job lost everything he had. He lost his children, his wealth, and his reputation. Even his wife turned on him and urged him to curse God and die.

Job is an example of a good man bad things happened to. Yet, the "just world" philosophy lived on in the hearts of his critics. All three of his friends who came to "comfort" him basically 'threw the book' at him, blaming him for his plight in life.

The "just world philosophy" also lives on in many hearts today. People are usually smart enough not to verbalize it, but the way they treat others whom they deem inferior to them or 'down and out' betrays them.

If we are sincere in wanting to make a difference in the lives of children, we should condemn and abandon the cruel "just world philosophy." Kids who are down and out or who aren't measuring up need to hear the right message.

Millions of people are driven by the idea that they must achieve, perform, earn, strive, fight, pull, and run at a fast pace in order to achieve status. That has caused havoc in relationships and sets people up to love others with major conditions. I don't think we deliberately set out to love people with conditions – especially kids – but that's how it all works out if we haven't fundamentally

---

Millions of people are driven by the idea that they must achieve, perform, earn, strive, fight, pull, and run at a fast pace in order to achieve status.

changed our view of success. Now it's true some people are lazy, don't want to work, and think the world owes them a living. They don't want to study, learn a trade, or pay their dues in preparing themselves to succeed. I say to those individuals, "don't expect anyone else to do for you what you can only do for your self, with God's help. Take responsibility!" This may sound contrary to what I've been saying but it's really the same issue dressed in different clothes.

Who says you can't achieve? Who says you can't make a good living? Who says you *have* to fail? With God all things are possible! Get motivated and stop making excuses. The gifts God has given you deposited at your birth are yours to use. Your greatest gift back to Him is turning those gifts into something great. Use them. Develop them. Believe in them. You are special! You can change! You will be a success!

Children need parents who are bold enough to break the cycle. It's not easy. No one can love others like God loves - with absolutely no conditions - but we need to understand, that *is* how God loves us and accepts us. Unless we begin walking in that direction, we will train our children to grow up and buy into the same philosophy we've entertained for years.

Does accepting the fact that God loves you without conditions change how you discipline? Yes and No. (We will cover that in another chapter.) Yet, accepting God's unconditional love changes the *way* we deal with the kids we discipline. Instead of hanging some terrible label on them because of their failure, we correct them and continue to love them.

If you have accepted the false notion that failure means you are a cipher, then it will effect the way you think, talk, and relate to authority, and how you will act *as* an authority. Coming away from these false ideas is a major step in beginning to motivate kids to succeed.

> *If children aren't allowed to fail, they can't succeed.*

If children aren't allowed to fail, they can't succeed. If every time they fail you make light of them, or get angry with them, or punish them, they will learn that they are not allowed to fail. A better way is to discipline them for breaking the rules, not killing them with your words.

It's o.k. to fail. You are forgiven when you ask God for it. The only way kids can succeed is to not fear failure. When you fear failure you give up trying.

How can kids escape the fear of failure? It would help if the adults around them didn't make such a big deal about their mess ups. That doesn't that mean adults can't correct or tell them they're wrong. Adults can relate to kids out of a new sense of freedom if they allow **themselves** to fail. That's a great thing to pass on to kids.

For years I've had the fear of failure. It has crippled me emotionally in so many ways. Believing in your self as created in God's image and loving your self is so critical to succeeding.

In summary, what is self-esteem and how is it developed? Is it defined by achievement, performance, good grades, good looks, an abundance of money, station in life, or family heritage? Is it all those positive thoughts and feelings you try to conjure up as a result of succeeding? No, self esteem doesn't exist as a result of these things. It's from above. No strings attached.

You might say, "I don't deserve this gift." The Old Testament tells of God's covenant with Abraham. God promised Abraham and the children of Israel the land of

Canaan. Funny thing, there were no required payments. There was no special reason and Abraham didn't even ask!

If you're familiar with the book of Exodus, you know the children of Israel did everything **but** deserve the Promised Land. They complained, doubted, disobeyed, murmured, fought with Moses, built a golden calf to worship, and basically did everything to get God ticked off. While it's true the first generation of wilderness wanderers failed to make it into the land, the next generation of Israelites did! They struggled but they believed in the value God placed on them.

It's hard for us to accept a gift sometimes. We want to work for it. We want to pay for it or justify receiving it. Nothing will change the fact that your self worth is a gift. Just receive it!

THE 3RD KEY TO SUCCESS MOTIVATION:

Accept yourself as a parent and love your children based on the free gift of love from God.

Authority is a good thing if it's the right kind of authority. It can be a living nightmare when it's the wrong kind.

CHAPTER 4

How does 'authority' interface with success?

The word "authority" evokes mixed emotions. Bad memories of unfair or abusive treatment by authorities who acted in uncharitable ways toward us have a way of settling in our subconscious for years, adversely affecting the way we relate to all authority.

Good memories of authorities being nice, kind, and fair give us a positive feeling about them and our way of relating to them is different. Everyone encounters authority from infancy and we form opinions about them early on.

Authority is ever with us. It never leaves. The way we perceive it profoundly influences the way we approach problems, how we manage our relationships, and whether or not we take responsibility for our actions or blame others.

Most people grow up in families where parents are in charge and tell kids what to do and that's good. A few years later, teachers join parents in telling kids what to do. Then after kids turn 18 they continue to encounter authority of all types in higher education, the legal system, the military, the church and in personal relationships.

Authority is a good thing if it's the right kind of authority. It can be a living nightmare when it's the wrong kind. We all know about destructive ill-used authority. We've experienced it in this generation. The abuse of authority can be devastating to adults, not to mention kids. Misuse of authority is destructive to the human personality. I frequently see it happen in the home. Abuse of authority causes major damage to a child's view of himself and his view of the world, setting up major road blocks to success in life. Children who have been abused grow up angry. There is way too much anger in our world. There are so many kids who need to get rid of anger, bitterness, and resentment in their hearts. They can only do that when they learn to forgive and accept the people God's placed in their lives to guide them.

It's relatively easy to develop a negative attitude toward authority because most of us tend to resent it, even when it's "good" authority. Our human nature steps up and says, "I want my way no matter what it costs." Yet, God gave us authority for our benefit. It doesn't have to be feared because it's part of His design to bless and protect us. My dad was fair with me most of the time in his discipline but there are thousands of kids who don't know what a normal family looks like. Kids often carry around within them deep emotional wounds that if not healed will cause stress, strained relationships, depression, and acting out violence.

Have you ever noticed it's always easier and more convenient to spot the faults in our authorities than it is to come to grips with our own failure? It's always easier to blame our authorities than to obey them. We just naturally resist authority.

When the children of Israel were following Moses through the desert, they saw flaws in Moses' character and exploited those flaws to their own advantage. They used what they perceived as his shortcomings for excuses to rebel." Listen to the account from the Bible about the children of Israel after the spies returned from exploring the Promised Land: "That night all the people of the community raised their voices and wept aloud. All the Israelites grumbled against Moses and Aaron, and the whole assembly said to them, "If only we had died in Egypt! Or in this desert! Why is the Lord bringing us to this land only to let us fall by the sword? Our wives and children will be taken as plunder. Wouldn't it be better for us to go back to Egypt?" And they said to each other, "We should choose a leader and go back to Egypt." Numbers 14:1-4

The Israelites were fed up with Moses! They didn't want him to be their leader anymore, even though **God Himself** had appointed and anointed him to lead them into the land of Canaan. They were afraid of the inhabitants but instead of owning up to it, they blamed Moses and Aaron. They began whining and complaining about Moses' and wanted to appoint someone else to lead them back to Egypt. They were feeling sorry for themselves and were very unhappy about the length of time it was taking to get into the land, though ironically it was their own grumbling and doubt that was keeping them out!

All night long they kept on crying, speaking against Moses, and coming up with question after question. Then "The whole assembly talked about stoning them." Numbers 14:10.

Don't we do similar things? When we see flaws in those who are in charge supposing to be good examples of authority, we often use their failure as our justification to throw off restraint or react against them. The Children of Israel's complaint was due to their "perceived" failure in leadership, in spite of the fact that Moses was doing everything right. It's always easier to complain about authority than to take personal responsibility for ourselves. Millions today 'write-off' authority or criticize it simply because they perceive faults, foibles, and failures in the authority over them. Those in authority among us ought to not be excused for making bad decisions but we who are under authority need to realize that authorities aren't perfect. Perfection is not a requisite for holding positions of power. We develop wrong concepts of authority when we base our reasons for listening to them on whether they're flawless. Based on poor role models, people rise up against authority and this attitude is passed on to the next generation, who pass it on to the next generation and they to the next generation and the next for many years. Poor role models in the home have caused massive confusion in our culture!

My concept of authority was formed early in my life by my dad.

When I was growing up, my dad would do all the talking at meal times. My brothers and sisters and I were to "be good" and listen. He would often remind us, "In my day, children were to be seen and not heard." Then he would drone on and on about stories we'd all heard a million times before without allowing anyone's word in edgewise.

As time passed, my dad's attitude and his habit of controlling all conversations began to take a major toll on our family's relationship. My brothers and sisters and I would all talk amongst ourselves about his manipulation and how we resented every minute of it. We didn't know to call it control at the time because we didn't realize that it **was** control. Yet, even my mother - living saint as she was - spoke in whispered tones outside about how despondent she felt around him when he would consume hour upon hour of talking her ear off.

As my brothers, sisters, and I grew older, we concluded that my dad was 'socially inept.' He was accustomed to just taking over a conversation and everyone else best prepare to hunker down for the long duration. Needless to say, people avoided him.

My dad was my first authority. I was not aware of it at the time, but

> *I didn't realize it until much later the real reason I sat and listened to my dad. I sat and listened in exchange for his approval.*

as I would sit and listen to my dad's monologues over and over again, my opinion of him and of authority in general, was taking a decided downward turn. When I was small, I had no choice but to listen and I was still too young to be in touch with what was really happening on the inside. As I got a little older, I would just feel guilty for fidgeting and wanting to get away.

As my older brothers and sisters began leaving home, I was the last one left, being the youngest. I would sit and listen for hours to my dad discuss things he had told me a dozen times before. I would leave our sessions feeling uneasy, small, and angry. I felt like I was caught on fly paper, but I still wasn't making the connection between what he was doing and what might be happening to me because of it.

I remember my mother once telling me that she had tried on several occasions to just sit and listen in hopes that dad would get 'talked out.' Well, in all my mom's attempts, she never wore him out, even after four and five hour marathons. My dad just never quit. He never did get 'talked out.' She finally gave up. She either would not talk to my dad, or get up in the middle of one of his sentences and say, "I've got a lot of things to do, Ken." and walk out.

No one had much choice. Whenever my dad would pause in a conversation, one might try to take a quick breath to say something, but he would continue talking before you could get the next word out. It seemed like my dad's sentences never ended. They were just one long run-on sentence connected with the word "a- n- d."

What kind of impact did that have on me?

I didn't realize it until much later the real reason I sat and listened to my dad. I sat and listened in exchange for his approval. Of course! He was my dad. He was very intelligent. He represented my security, wisdom, heritage, and well being. I learned that if I listened to him for a while, I could usually manage to slip away with a bathroom excuse and still garner his approval. Before I left, he would graciously acknowledge what a 'good boy' I was for my interest and give me an off handed compliment for my attentiveness and sensitivity. Secretly for me though, it turned into an endurance test as I watched the grass grow under my feet.

When I finally realized his never ending monologues were a permanent monument engraved in the past, I began walking away earlier and earlier from our conversations. I would interrupt his thoughts, later feeling guilty, but not for long. My determination to escape grew more intense than my need for his nod of acceptance.

A pastor and colleague in ministry once said to me, "Do you know that new janitor around the church?" "Yes", I said knowingly, "You have to be rude to him to break away from his conversations." He said.

In order to break away from my father's control, I had to be rude. There was just no other way.

What kind of impact did this have on me? After I became an adult in my twenties, I noticed that whenever I would talk to an authority figure, I would walk away feeling like a little boy. I would freeze up. I couldn't think. I felt I needed to listen, listen, listen, and not say a word, yet I would feel more and more uncomfortable the longer the conversation continued. I struggled for years with intimidation of those over me, including senior pastors of the churches I served as youth or associate pastor.

It could have all been so different!

> *Dad's have more influence on their children than they often stop to consider.*

> *There's nothing more kids need from fathers and mothers than their approval.*

Dad's have more influence on their children than they often stop to consider. I felt paralyzed inside when my dad would imprison me in his conversations. I developed a clinical depression when I was 19 and wanted to take my own life. I did not develop a healthy self esteem and would feel immobilized whenever I tried to talk.

My dad was well intentioned. I believe he loved me. Yet, instead of instilling in me value and respect, he deposited fear and a warped concept of authority. He could have helped so much by just respecting me, respecting my time, my wants and wishes. He could have helped me so much by simply allowing me to be a man like him.

At his memorial I came to the funeral home early to have a private alone time with him at his casket. I was so hurt, but it was only then that I could really express it. I said to him as he laid silent and still, "Dad, why couldn't you have just noticed me for me, and talked to me in a way that included me, a worthy son. Why didn't you listen to me?"

I have forgiven my dad.

He did his best and I'm not his judge. He was a good provider. He taught me many things to prepare me for my life and I love him.

There's nothing more kids need from fathers and mothers than their approval. How can parents give approval if they undermine everything a child says or does by talking over them? How can parents give approval without words of appreciation, or without time to listen to them or have respect for their feelings? Parents ought to be sensitive to the feelings of their children even if they're three years old.

Parents often don't stop and put themselves in the

shoes of their kids. For example, when a mom has a bad hair day, woe to the person who looks cross-eyed at her! What about when a little girl has a bad hair day? A parent might say, "Oh it's no big deal. Get over it!"

Question? How is it any different for a little girl with a bad hair day who doesn't think she looks good, than for the mom who is grumpy all day because her hair is out of place?

Dad, if you were embarrassed at work because you didn't know something, how is it any different for your son when he is put on the spot at school for his ignorance on a particular subject? Yet, often when children complain about how frustrated they are in similar experiences, parents and teachers dismiss them with, "Oh, don't worry about it, you're focusing on the wrong thing." Instead, parents and teachers should take the time to lead kids through the steps of dealing adequately with their struggles and negative emotions.

Much has been written about the positive effects of affirmation and praise given to kids. I couldn't agree more. Kids succeed more when they are praised than when they are criticized. As we are growing up, the authorities in our lives have so much power to build or destroy. Research shows that the primary source of children's self esteem is derived from their father. If dad does not bestow a sense of dignity upon his children, they may never get it! This sets up impediments later to healthy relationships and a sound belief in oneself. It hampers success in life.

Sometimes we just need to get back to basics. In order for parents to impart the skills for kids to succeed, it's

Sometimes we just need to get back to basics.

> *There are few things that bring more freedom of choice, freedom of action, or more autonomy than ownership.*

important for them to have an understanding of true authority to pass on to their kids.

Why is authority important? Where does it come from? How we get it?

Webster's dictionary defines authority as, "the power to require and receive submission: the right to expect obedience: superiority derived from a status that carries with it the right to command and give final decisions."

We're all required to respond to authority in some way. There is authority at home, in the church, in government, and on the job. There is even authority in places we wish there wasn't, like the IRS.

Nevertheless, authority is.

Authority was here before you were born and authority will be here when you're gone.

It's extremely critical to a child's development for parents to first hold a healthy view of authority themselves in order to impart it to their kids. This may require parents first ironing out their own relationship to authority before imparting generational baggage to their kids. Did you despise your dad's control over you? Did you resent your mom?

If you want to impart the "gift of succeeding" to your children, you have to first check your own relationship with authority and come to terms with what really happened in your heart at home and other places when you encountered authority, good or bad.

Let's briefly discuss the origin of authority.

THERE ARE 3 SOURCES OF AUTHORITY:

#1 Ownership   #2 Knowledge   #3 Delegation

The first source of authority is ***ownership.***

What gives you the right to hire a gardener for your yard, choose a mechanic for your car, or allow a doctor to operate on you? What gives you authority to make choices about your future, your finances, or your career? Is it not **ownership?**

Ownership gives you full rights over what you hold in possession. Ownership gives you the right to call the shots. If I owned A.T.&T, I would have a lot of power. Could I not walk into a board meeting, express what I wanted and get it?

If you own something, you can lend it to others, you can lease it out, or you can have someone else look after it. You're in control when you're the owner. There are few things that bring more freedom of choice, freedom of action, or more autonomy than ownership. Authority that comes from ownership puts you in control. It releases power.

Ownership means that no one else has a right over what you own. No one can legally take what is yours or dictate what happens to what is yours. To own something means you legally have all the rights to it. Ownership gives you great authority. (By the way, I'm not covering here the Biblical concept of stewardship or management).

"Ownership" of a position or role of authority also gives you certain rights to expect submission and obedience, as in a military setting or in law enforcement. If I hold a position of authority, it gives me the right to make commands and give final decisions.

Ownership then, is the first source of authority. It's very basic to human dignity and to the free exercise of authority.

The second source of authority is ***knowledge***.

If you became seriously ill, would you depend on the next door neighbor's diagnosis for treatment? Probably not. You're not going to trust old wives tales or folk remedies when your life is on the line. You

> *It's possible to know all the facts about a particular subject – but not apply it to anything practical – and therefore fail.*

would not take a chance with your health on a whim. You want a professional diagnosis from a trained physician who is legally obligated to you if he missteps. So, it's the doctor's **knowledge** that gives him authority.

A doctor is allowed to practice medicine because he has passed a rigorous set of standards. He has gone to school, served an internship, and has passed exams. He is paid to give you the right information and is liable if he fails. That's what gives him the power to make decisions about your health, with your permission or course.

Power flows from knowing. When you know something, it puts you at the helm. When you know something, it gives you the right to be right! I'm not talking about exercising authority because you think you know, or because you assume you know. Someone has said; opinions are the cheapest commodities on planet earth. That's not the kind of knowledge I'm talking about. I'm talking about knowledge that is correct and accurate about things over which important decisions are made. I'm talking about knowing the answers to problems when the solutions are not obvious.

If kids are going to succeed, it's vital they understand that ***true authority comes from knowing.***

It's important here to mention some other dimensions of knowledge. Knowledge by itself is limited. If authority is to be released properly and appropriately, knowledge must be rooted in the practical and in a person's character. That kind of knowledge goes far beyond knowing facts.

To 'know' something is only the beginning. One must also get in touch with the real world of not only knowing something, but ***doing*** it. Unless you ***do*** it, you don't ***know*** it. The Bible says, "Do not merely listen to the word, and so deceive yourselves. Do what it says." James 1:22. The person who thinks he knows something, but does not do it, deceives himself. You are living in an illusory world if you think you know something but don't practice it. As a matter of fact, if you fail to do something with the knowledge you have, your knowledge is useless.

It's possible to know all the facts about a particular subject – but not apply it to anything practical - and therefore fail. For example, it's possible to earn a Ph.D. in business administration and be an abysmal failure at business. It's possible to have a degree in construction and be a poor builder.

Possessing knowledge but not applying it is tragically demonstrated in our world everyday. Just look at our politicians. Character means something! It makes a difference in the outcome of families, churches, businesses, and nations. Each of the following examples is true. How about the stock market broker who was making huge profits by cheating his clients? He was imprisoned for a pounce scheme that cost his clients billions of dollars. How about the city manager who pilfered millions of dollars from the city fund? How about the attorney's who bilked millions of dollars from their clients by lying about the settlement amounts from a pharmaceutical company? We find examples like this almost daily. There are financial planners who go bankrupt, attorneys sent to prison for cheating on their taxes, and ministers who lose their ministries over sexual indiscretions.

So there are different levels of knowing. We say we "know" the postman to whom we say "hello" to everyday. We say we "know" someone when we know about their likes and dislikes. The Bible uses phrases like "Adam knew his wife." These are not all the same kinds of "knowing." 'Knowing' has different levels. We all "know" the president of the U.S., but we don't really "know" him. The highest level of "knowing" is experiencing first hand what you know.

It's incredibly important that children learn the difference between just knowing the facts about something versus having an emotional commitment to make decisions regarding their "knowing." Strong authority has the ability to **act** on knowledge and that only happens through moral fortitude and character.

Numerous examples could be given to demonstrate how knowledge, skill, ability, and intelligence fall far short of making someone a good leader. Moral strength is needed in the mix if authority is to be used effectively! Everyday we read about people who know right from wrong but choose the wrong. Why? Because they simply don't have the power to do what's right.

A few years ago, the corporate heads of Enron **knew** what was right yet embezzled millions of dollars of investors' money. Catholic priests **knew** it was immoral to molest young boys but did it anyway. Not just a few of our Presidents **knew** what was right but ordered break-ins, lied, obstructed justice, and deceived the American public.

Men and women may attain to a place of authority because of their knowledge, skill, and abilities but then misuse their authority because they lack moral fortitude. True authority comes from moral strength, not simply skill, ability, intelligence, or knowledge.

The third source of authority is ***delegation***.

Delegation is defined as "as a person authorized to act for another, to entrust to another." We all understand what this entails. It simply means someone who already has authority gives it to someone else.

Delegation is just as important to teach kids as authority itself. Delegation is taught by giving it, not by talking about it. Giving authority away to kids in appropriate proportions to match their age and maturity is essential for their growth. Successful churches, companies, restaurants, governments, and homes, all delegate authority.

For kids to grow into mature, capable, and successful adults, they must be given bits of delegated authority as they grow in greater and greater amounts. It stunts our growth for someone to undervalue our potential, to limit us, to stifle our dreams, or be told we're not ready or that we're inept because someone refuses to let go of control. We all like being in control because it feels good. I wish sometimes I could control the whole world, but I can't. I've learned in business, ministry, and at home, I have to delegate authority if I'm going to retain my sanity and be successful.

Mom and dad, if you want to teach responsibility to your children, then delegate responsibility. If you want to teach a good work ethic, then delegate chores. If you want to teach respect, then respect the authority you've delegated to your children be allowing them to fail. How else will kids ever become persons of authority?

It's amazing how many homes I've been in where the kids have literally been disabled by parents who don't delegate anything meaningful to them. They treat their kids as if they are lame, retarded, and an embarrassment to the family name. Of course your kids won't do the job as excellent as you, but when are they going to learn? Let go.

I've paid my own dues for delegating authority.

One day I told my son Rob to trim the Juniper bushes in front of our mobile home. I didn't feel the need to give him instructions. I assumed he knew what to do. It wasn't hard, right? When he was finished I went out front and looked. I gasped out loud. "Oh my gosh, what was I thinking?" He hacked the bushes so severely it took months for them to recover.

On another occasion, Rob wanted to start an auto detailing business. I thought it was a great idea. I bought him all the needed supplies and talked to him - as much as a thirteen year old will allow - about what he should do. I was satisfied with his apparent level of competence until one day there came a loud knock at our door. I answered only to see a very angry man standing in front of me. "Are you Mr. Teel?" the inquiry came rather forcefully. "Yes, I am," I said, "Is there a problem?" "Well," he paused, "I hired your son to wash my new BMW and he used a Brillo pad on the hood." "What!," I wheezed. "Where is the car?" Sure enough, my son wasn't able to remove the tree sap on the hood with a sponge so he used a wire cleaning pad on the man's brand new beautiful beamer! That "delegation" cost me $350.00, split between me and the father of my son's friend who was helping.

I can laugh now. Looking back I realize I could have done a better job of explaining what and what not to do when washing a car and monitor his activity just a little bit more carefully!

Understanding and properly relating to authority is **extremely** important for kids to learn very early. If kids don't learn how to respond to authority at home, woe to those parents and to everyone else around them!

By the way, what style of authority are your children learning from you? Are they learning from a dictator who uses a 'scorched earth' approach to leadership? Are they learning that their authority never means what it says or never follows through or never makes good on promises? Are they learning that authority is inconsistent, soft on discipline, or wishy-washy?

Kids will emulate the kinds of strengths and flaws they are exposed to by their parents, not necessarily what they're told. Perhaps you never had a good example growing up and now you're a parent. Maybe you don't know how to relate in a truly healthy way to your own kids. It's never too late. Begin now by humbling yourself before God. Admit where you've been wrong. Search for understanding about how you can change your own attitude. When parents' attitude toward authority is right then they can be the right kind of authority to their kids.

Before we can be "in authority," we must first learn to be "under authority." Perhaps you're having difficulty today imparting good things to your kids because you were impaired by the bad authorities in your life. The good news is, you **can** change when you realize that all authority comes from God and humbly accept your place under Him.

It's easy to see the connection between the origin of authority and God. He has all authority because He owns all things and knows all things. Therefore, all true authority comes from Him.

> *Kids will emulate the kinds of strengths and flaws they are exposed to by their parents, not necessarily what they're told.*

THE 4th KEY TO SUCCESS MOTIVATION:

Teach children the true origin of authority and how to use it.

> *Countless authorities have miserably failed us - from the top down.*

CHAPTER 5

WHATEVER BECAME OF 'SUBMISSION TO AUTHORITY?'

Authority of all types in our culture have severely declined in strength and credibility over the past few decades.

Countless authorities have miserably failed us - from the top down. We are now a culture who is paying a great price for these "authorities" misdeeds. Authorities on all levels - government, church, home, and school - have managed to create huge credibility gaps by doing and being the exact opposite of who they said they were, and doing everything *but* what they were suppose to do.

Here are but a few examples:
- ◊ The largest and costliest scandal in world history occurred under the United Nations' watch during the Iraqi "Food for Oil" program.
- ◊ Who could have imagined a standing president of the United States engaging in sexual indecencies in the White House?

- ◊ Who would have believed numerous U.S. presidents routinely lying or killing to cover up the truth?
- ◊ Who could have guessed a well known and respected evangelist's addictions to sex, money, and fame?
- ◊ Who could have predicted Wall Street's repeated malfeasance too vast to innumerate?
- ◊ And the list goes on and on…

What about our public schools?

The authority breakdown in our educational system dropped to a new low when many school teachers around the country decided to have sex with their students. Sexual conquests on high school campuses have spun out of control with boys on some schools campuses having sexual intercourse with more than 25 different girls. Girls are now offering oral sex to boys they think are cute in middle school. Metal detectors are an all too familiar scene on many campuses, fostered by the Columbine High School Tragedy in Colorado.

Fathers have burned their houses down with their families in it. Mothers have drowned their own children. It's a tragic and a truly sad reality that 'authority' has totally lost its way. Those we trusted betrayed us, hurt us, lied to us, and abandoned us.

I think there used to be in the early 60's - when I was growing up - a kind of automatic respect for authority. That no longer exists. Authorities we wanted to trust let us down the most. I think that's why multitudes have become cynical toward authority even when the authority is good. But here's our dilemma with authority: if authority becomes our enemy, to whom can we turn? Is it any wonder our culture is sinking into a quagmire of moral confusion?

Giving up on authority is very tempting. We've all rebelled against it at some point in time, whether or not the authority was good or bad.

The Bible calls that sin, and we have **all** sinned. "For all have sinned and fall short of the glory of God." Romans 3:23

The truth is, as much as we might like to think of ourselves as liberated, we can't do without authority. The world wouldn't work without it. We still need authority, if only to help life run smoothly. The latter half of the twentieth century and first part of the 21st century has found mankind trying life without authority. The result? The suffering of great loss. God designed authority structure and we're not able live in peace without it.

What is the right structure authority? It's actually quite simple. I've said it before, God owns everything, knows everything, and has power to do whatever He wants, so that makes Him the primary source of all authority. The good news is, He is an awesome God who has compassion and understands justice, has mercy; and is the lover of our souls. He wants things to go well for us.

The path to success is to understand how and where God has delegated His authority and intelligently submit to it. Success is only possible when we have an understanding of who is control and who should be in control. God has first delegated all authority to Christ. "For by him were all things created: things in heaven and on earth, visible and invisible, whether thrones or power or rulers or authorities; all things are created by him and for him. He is before all things, in him all things hold together. And he is the head of the body, the church, he is the beginning and the firstborn from among the dead, so that in everything he might have

---

The truth is, as much as we might like to think of ourselves as liberated, we can't do without authority.

The path to success is to understand how and where God has delegated His authority and intelligently submit to it.

the supremacy." Colossians 1:15-18. Christ in turn has delegated His authority to three main areas on earth: the **church**, the **home**, and **government.**

CHURCH: "It was he (Christ) who gave some to be apostles, some to be prophets, some to be evangelists, and some to be pastors and teachers." Ephesians 4:11

HOME: "Children, obey your parents in the Lord, for this is right. Honor your father and mother – which is the first commandment with a promise – that it may go well with you and that you may enjoy long life on the earth." Ephesians 6:1, 2

GOVERNMENT: "Everyone must submit himself to the governing authorities, for there is no authority except that which God has established." Romans 13:1

When you explain this to your kids, watch them change! When they gain an understanding of *why* they are submitting to authority, not simply because "you said so," their attitudes will do a u-turn.

Good examples and effective living begins when grown ups understand and relate in healthy ways to authority themselves and then model that to kids.

When kids are shown *why* they need to listen and humble themselves under authority, there will be a radical change in how they relate to you. Without this breakthrough, there will be an uphill battle for parents, teachers and any other authority. Without learning this, kids later on will find themselves at odds with the law or with an officer in the military, or with a boss on their job.

> *When kids are shown why they need to listen and humble themselves under authority, there will be a radical change in how they relate to you.*

How can you change kids attitude toward authority?

Have you ever noticed that making stricter rules for rebellious kids almost never works?

You can't just make rules bigger and stronger and restrictions harder and more intrusive and not expect kids to dig in their heals at your attempt to bring order. You can't lock them in their rooms and make your home a prison. It doesn't work. Kids need to understand **why** they should listen to authority, not shouted at to "do it or else." Kids are a lot like us, they are more likely to give in when they want to. "Wanting to give in" comes from a deep understanding of where authority comes from and how it works.

Finding the purpose behind submission to authority then, is a major key in helping kids get through the rebellious stages and on into the successful stages. The purpose behind submitting to authority is building relationships.

When we were kids, God gave us parents to love, relate to, and submit to. That's the way of life. God's long range intention for mankind is to understand who He is and that it's His prerogative to make judgments and decisions about all things.

To reveal Himself, God has delegated His authority through the church, home, and government to bless the earth and mankind. He reveals His authority through these channels so that we may know the reason **behind** authority. It doesn't make sense to teach kids anything else.

"Submission" has become a bad word. Yet, submission is a good thing, not bad. Life would not run well if no one

To reveal Himself, God has delegated His authority through the church, home, and government to bless the earth and mankind.

submitted to anyone else. Without submission businesses would fail, government offices shut down, homes self destruct, churches vanish, and public safety become a nightmare.

Let's suppose two men were appointed to run a large corporation. Both were given different job descriptions but held the exact same authority. Everything went fine until one day the company found itself at a crossroads. The two men vehemently disagreed about what to do. When they tried to communicate they came away from their conversations more entrenched in their own thinking than ever before. After many attempts at negotiating, they still couldn't seem to agree and compromise was not an option.

What could these men do? One of them could quit, leaving the other with full authority. They could both agree to split the company in half and both go in the direction they think best, separately. Or, one of them could give in to the other. One of them could say, "I'll try it your way." Whatever they decide, they must do something, or progress will be impeded, financial losses sustained, or worse, failure of the company could be at stake.

Can you see how submission might be necessary to save the company? This is almost a daily scenario around the world. This is also a picture of what happens in many marriages, schools, government or other institutions who can't see their way clear to a compromise. Submission is an important part of all of our lives and even a key to survival at times.

Why is it then so difficult to submit? We're human. We've got pride, rebellion, and a mind of our own. When it comes to kids, can you see how we must first be in submission before we can be teachers of submission? The Apostle Paul said, "And the things you have heard me say in the presence of many witnesses entrust to **reliable men who will also be qualified to teach other.**" II Timothy 2:2

> *Being smart doesn't mean you can make good decisions.*

Have you noticed a lot of unwise and incompetent people in authority? Possessing authority doesn't make you right. Being smart doesn't mean you can make good decisions.

What about delegated authority?

When a parent leaves a child with a babysitter, words like these are often exchanged. "Now, Johnny, you obey her. I will be asking her how you behaved." And to the babysitter, words like these are said, "I want you to tell me if Johnny acts up. I give you permission to send him to his room, turn off the T.V., or put him to bed."

That's delegated authority. We encounter it everyday. It would seem delegated authority is a weaker form of pure authority, but is it?

Take the power of attorney for instance. The power of attorney is just as powerful as if the person themselves were present to execute the plans. When authority is given through delegation, delegated authority represents the authority just as if the authority were present.

This is a powerful concept kids can use to effect positive change. Leaders who neglect or refuse to delegate authority lose leadership in whatever arena of life they're involved in.

Kids need to learn about delegated authority in order to become good leaders. How do they learn it? By being given age-appropriate responsibility. By being trusted. No one can become successful if they aren't trusted and given opportunities to develop.

Learning to follow the three sources of authority given to us is necessary for us to lead successful lives. It's also necessary for kids to understand the relationships behind authority that make it work. Authority does not exist in a vacuum.

Everything rises and falls on authority. It's crucial that children understand how important authority is if they are going to grow into healthy, strong adults. If children ever give us peace by listening to our authority without resistance and resentment, it's because 'right' authority has been imparted to them.

Kids *can* be taught to respect authority. They can be shown how authority may not always be right but to approach it respectfully. They can be taught how to make an appeal to authority.

I taught my kids to respect me. I also taught them I was not always right and how to approach me if they thought I was wrong. I taught them how to make an appeal to authority. If parents would allow their kids to approach them, they would find disciplining so much easier when kid's seem to be acting in defiance.

One day my son's friend Jim asked me for help. He told me he was having nothing but trouble with the teachers at his high school. I asked him to give an example.

He said, "Well, this one teacher is always singling me out and embarrassing me in front of the entire class." I said, "Tell me why you think this is happening." He said, "I don't know, but when I think she is wrong about something I stand up to her in class."

I said, "What do you mean, stand up to her?" He said, "Well, I tell her when I think she is wrong about something and that she should do something about it right then and there."

I said, "Jim, did you know you are breaking the basic rules of how to appeal to an authority?" He said, "What are you talking about?" I said, "Well, for instance, do you really think it's the right time to tell her you think she is wrong in the middle of her class?" He sheepishly said, "I guess not, but if I don't say something, I'll be humiliated by her." I said,

> *Learning to effectively request a hearing from authority is one of the most important things kids can add to their box of tools for coping.*

"Maybe she is targeting you because you are offending her by confronting her in the middle of class."

I proceeded to share with Jim the right and wrong ways to approach authority. I told him in the middle of class is not the right time to confront his teacher. I said, "Try going to her when she is not busy and you have her complete undivided attention." I said, "This is the first step, right timing." "Then humbly tell her that you respect her as your teacher and want to guard her reputation." That's the second step, right attitude." "Then tell her how you have been embarrassed and hurt by what she has said to you in class."

I shared with Jim the various steps to take and he used them! A couple of weeks later he came to me all excited, "Hey Ken, you know that teacher I was telling you about? I said, "Yes." He said, "Everything is better now. I did what you told me and now the problem is solved and I'm getting a better grade in her class." "Amazing!" I exclaimed, "I'm really happy you learned the right way to approach authority."

It *was* amazing – such little time spent with Jim for such incredible results!

Learning to effectively request a hearing from authority is one of the most important things kids can add to their box of tools for coping. It's one of the most important things parents can do for their kids to prepare them for the passage between childhood and adulthood.

Some parents view their children as possessions to be manipulated, controlled, and dominated. Those involved with kids need to consider the feelings of kids and treat them with respect. They need to prepare them for the transition to maturity. The sooner you begin to view your children as "pre-adult," the better off everyone will be.

Dads ought to be thinking about how to help their sons become men - and when they become young men - welcome them into the adult world. Moms ought to be thinking about how they're going to help her daughters become women. It's not common that dads and moms give permission to sons and daughters to be on their level. Parents are too busy trying to be "in charge" or trying be "right" to allow their children that privilege, consequently, a lot of good communication is lost and hence understanding between kids and parents goes out the window.

There never came a day with own dad when I was on his level. There was always an unseen wall - his position – and my inferior position. He was dad, I was a child. You would think that by the time I reached 40 he would give me a little respect. I'm sure he tried but he never quite arrived at that point.

Imparting good authority is everything. We all model some paradigm of authority. Is it the right one? To be a good authority, you may have to change the way you view yourself. Are you Mr. or Mrs. "know-it-all?" Are you "always right?" Are you unapproachable? Or are you humble enough to admit your mistakes?

For your kids to have a pleasant experience with authority, you may have to change the way you view them. Are they a nuisance? Are they in the way? Are they witless sapheads? You need to remind yourself over and over, these are *my* kids and they're a lot like me! For approximately 18 years, I will be preparing them for independence. Have I been showing them for years leading up to age 18 little by little a kind, compassionate, and just, form of authority, or are am I teaching them a cruel, impatient, controlling form of authority? Either

> *Parent's ought not use their authority for their own convenience.*

way, I and they will be reaping the consequences many times over.

I used to tell my kids, "You know what?" "You are sixteen." "In less than three years you'll be making adult decisions on your own. It's probable that you will meet your life partner in the next three years. It's probable that you will make a decision about your life's career in the next three years. It's probable that you will be faced with supporting yourself in the next three years. In the next three years, you will be making decisions without me. Savor these years you have with me because childhood is fleeting, just like life. Don't resent that I still have a lot of control over your life. Be thankful because in the not too distant future, everything will change.

Children need to be treated with respect. Parents need to look ahead. Dad and Mom, your daughter who seems to be taking forever to grow up in your home will soon be leaving. "But she's only fourteen," you say. Well, in four short years she could be married. Are you preparing her? Or are you 'keeping her under your thumb?' Do you restrict her every move? Are you limiting her decision making about things that directly involve her?

It's important to clarify what kind of authority parents operate from. It's a place of **delegated** authority. It does not flow out of knowledge (who knows how to raise kids before they raise them?) and it does not flow out of ownership (you just think your kids belong to you).

It's important to consider and keep fresh in our memories that we are parents by delegation from God.

Parent's ought not use their authority for their own convenience. Parents aren't owners of children, they are temporary stewards. A steward is someone who takes care of someone else's property. Children are a gift from God to guide for a few short years, that's it. Make those years count! Make them positive. Make them constructive and enjoyable. Stop and think about your children's feelings. Don't ignore what's important to your children simply because it's not important to you. Live what you believe before your children - don't worry - they ***will*** pick up on it! They will more likely adopt your value system by watching you than by you preaching to them about it.

    Show your kids a better way of doing things. ***Show*** them a better way of thinking. For their sakes, patiently ***show*** them where they're wrong. Don't condemn them for their short-sightedness. That's what parents are for, to help children see the bigger picture.

THE 5TH KEY TO SUCCESS MOTIVATION:

Model and impart 'good' authority to kids.

CHAPTER 6

How does child discipline fit into success motivation?

"Do not withhold discipline from a child; if you punish him with the rod, he will not die. Punish him with the rod and save his soul from death." Proverbs 23:13, 14

Some people think that spanking their child is going to hurt them or damage their psyche. Nothing could be further from the truth!

Sure, effective discipline is going to cause a child pain temporarily. It's suppose too! It will pay off later. Discipline done correctly is going to save your child's life in the long run. It will sting and hurt, and they may cry, but that's better than your child's death wouldn't you agree?

This is serious! Parents, the Bible is always right. According to these verses if you use the rod you will save your child's soul from death. This reference also says, if you discipline with the rod, he will not die and this means both physical and spiritual death. This is a matter of life and death! It's worth it to take action and discipline children lovingly and effectively.

I've seen firsthand many ineffective methods of child rearing employed by parents which are absolutely heartbreaking. In one very well-appointed home where I had the privilege of teaching, both parents were physicians.

When I first began teaching in this home, the father in a rough, guttural voice would command the boys indoors for their lessons. After rushing in, they were met with the demand, "What took you so long? This was followed by a long barrage of accusations about keeping the teacher waiting, questions about why they hadn't practiced, why one brother was bothering the other, and why they weren't listening, all acted out by the father with a strong, vociferous voice.

I couldn't help but notice the boys' body language - so revealing – arched back, chiseled face, anger seething just under the surface, making excuses for anything and everything. They found it difficult to focus on the lessons, resisting me as they resisted their dad. To make matters worse, the mom worked 12 hours a day so there was no time for housework or kids. Had careers replaced caring? I don't know and I'm not the judge. I believe both parents loved their kids. They were trying their best but I think were surely confused about how to show their love.

One might think that in a home such as this you would find children brought up in a healthier way. We would all hope so. Unfortunately, popular and widespread misconceptions have changed the true meaning of discipline.

What often passes off as discipline in many homes is simply parents yelling at kids. There's no true discipline, only intolerant and impatient reactions of someone's frustration or the outbursts of an irritated mom or dad venting anger over repressed feelings of powerlessness. Parents need to stop and think about the impact their words and actions are having on their kids. Our words are powerful and far-reaching.

The good news about the home mentioned above is the situation began to slowly change. The dad began to soften up. I think he realized that "a little honey is better than straight vinegar." I say humbly but truthfully, he saw the difference in my teaching. Patience, words of kindness, and treating students with respect made a huge difference in the boys' attitudes as well as their progress on the piano!

In another home where I was invited to teach, the mom was a pediatrician, the dad an attorney. After our first lesson, the eight- year-old son decided to continue playing the piano after his dad requested he go into another room while we discussed the music business policy. I found myself slowly raising my voice to overcome the ever- increasing volume of his piano banging. When the father took no action to correct this unknowingly rude behavior on the part of the boy, I turned to the boy smiling and said, "Your lesson is over so you can go into the other room and play." Nothing doing. He was going to stay.

There we sat. The dad a big, intelligent, strong young man, stymied and controlled by his eight-year-old son, unable to persuade him to be considerate or respect the wishes of his new teacher or father. We were sitting there at the mercy of a eight-year-old! I think we all know this, but discipline or the lack thereof, can build children up or it can pulverize them. I know you are interested in the kind of discipline that builds or you wouldn't be reading this book.

Real love is tough. It stands up for truth and doesn't bend in compromise. It perseveres until it prevails.

One day, Jessie's mom was not happy with what he was doing. When she came near to talk to him, he shouted, "don't touch me!" The mother then stepped away silently in complete submission to her 7 year old son's command.

What's wrong with that picture? You might say, "I'd never let that happen to me." Well, it is tragic to say there are thousands of parents who are letting it happen everyday. Many parents have effectively given away all control to their children.

Some parents feel that "little Jessie" needs to feel what it's like to get what he wants so why should an adult stand in his way, even his parents? This is the flip side of the coin of what we we've talked about in previous chapters about giving kids dignity and respect.

"Little Jessie" doesn't know it, but someone needs to say "no" to him and make it stick. "Little Jessie" needs boundaries, not unbridled liberty. Kids need to be shown that there are consequences for bad decisions.

Don't we already know this? It's a horrible mistake to give kids anything they want anytime they want it. Real love is tough. It stands up for truth and will not bend for compromise. It perseveres until it prevails.

When my kids, Robby, Ryan, and Alison were growing up, I tried to pay very close attention to where they were and what they were doing.

I'll never forget one day when Robby, now a young teen, failed to come home at our 3 PM agreed time. I waited another 15 minutes to give him grace. At 3:15 I began calling around to his friends to see if I could find him. After a long search with no luck, I got concerned. My concern slowly turned to annoyance, then anger. I called some more. No Robby. I drove down to the local theatre. When I walked up to the door, the usher saw my expression and decided not to ask any questions. He let me right in when I told him I was there to look for my son. I searched every movie theatre. No Robby. By this time I was thinking something bad had happened. I tried not to dwell on the negative. The nagging thought of his inconsideration and disobedience was battling against the thought of a possible tragedy. Though I could not find him right then, I didn't call the police.

Robby came back that night at 9 PM. I had plenty of time to think so I prepared his sleeping bag and some snacks and laid them on the back stairs outside. I told him, "You have lost the privilege of staying here." Then I said goodbye and closed the door.

Too harsh? Perhaps.

I'm not advocating anyone do what I did. Frankly, I didn't know what else to do. He was a young teen who had pushed the envelope one too many times. I didn't know of any other way to get the message through to him. I was relatively sure he would spend the night with his friend and that was a comforting enough thought to allow me some sleep.

That was Friday night. Sunday night he called and asked me if he could come home. I said, "Are you willing to obey the rules of the house?" "Yes," he said. "OK then, come home son." I urged. I watched and waited for him with high levels of anticipation. At that point I was feeling pretty guilty about kicking him out. When the door swung open, I ran up and put both arms around him. I smothered him with a big, long hug and said, "I'm so glad you're home, son." He answered, "Me too dad, me too."

Rob never repeated that. He needed limits.

In chapter 1 I said self-esteem is God's gift based on His unconditional love. That's true, but there's a huge difference between loving a child unconditionally and going squishy on bad behavior.

Unconditional love is not the absence of boundaries. Actually, it's the presence of boundaries that keep relationships safe. Unconditional love is not promiscuity or the absence of accountability. Unconditional love does not take a passive approach to real problems or treat lightly

there's a huge difference between loving a child unconditionally and going squishy on bad behavior.

the issues kids are facing. Love builds protective fences. Love expects others to take responsibility for their actions.

If you grew up in a home where excessive authority was hung over your head each and every minute, you might be emotionally overreacting now with your own kids by engaging in an "anything goes" attitude. Perhaps you grew up under an abusive authority that hurt you so you have consciously or subconsciously decided you're not going to let that happen in your home. If you were hurt or offended as a child, it's easy go to the other extreme.

Let's go back to where authority comes from. All authority comes from God. God has given His authority for parents to raise their children. Authority *is* needed when we're growing up - the right kind of authority. Not abusive authority. Not promiscuous authority.

I would like to outline a simple way of disciplining kids from day one and impart to them what they need to know to succeed. They don't have to be abused, violated, stifled, or yelled at to show them the truth.

The book of Proverbs says, "Foolishness in bound in the heart of a child, but the rod of correction will drive it far from him." Proverbs 22:15 (KJV)

It's my firm conviction that corporal discipline is necessary in the lives of children beginning at age two or three. If parents could come to some sort of agreement about consequences for bad behavior, they would be miles ahead of the game. Discipline ought to be quick, decisive, painful, but measured. "Measured discipline" means age appropriate discipline that fits the extent of bad behavior. "Painful discipline" means discipline that hurts but does not injure. The object of discipline is to **train kids to both listen and respond to the word of their parent's authority.**

Having said that, it's my firm conviction discipline be built on principles rather than rules. For example, it may not be wrong for kids to play in the living room, but it may be wrong if company is over. Teaching kids principles over rules means they understand, it's ok sometimes and other times it's not ok. The difference is respecting a parent's judgment rather than adhering to a hard and fast rule.

Proverbs 22:6 says, "Train a child in the way he should go, and when he is old, he will not turn from it." Training is huge. You are training your child to listen. Listening is a key component to success. The parent's part is to make, wise, kind, and firm decisions. The child's part is to hear those decisions and respond. It's not rocket science. It's all in the way it's done. It reminds me of the story of the mom who came into the bedroom full of kids one day and said, "Would someone go clean up the kitchen!" No one moved. Everyone **heard** what she said, but no one ***listened.*** But then again, there was no one in the room with the name of 'someone!' You have to be specific!

Training is more than instruction. Have you ever trained a dog? You throw the stick and shout, "Go get it!" If he doesn't fetch it, you throw it again or pick up the stick, put it in his mouth and run with him. If you do this enough times, eventually the dog will fetch the stick.

In a similar fashion, training a child may require you to go over and over what you want them to do. It's not just teaching, teaching falls short. Becoming involved in the process of demonstrating what you expect and walking them through the steps with encouraging words makes it effective.

If you are consistent with training, it <u>will</u> work. Be patient. It may not seem like you're making headway now, but somewhere in the future your training ***will*** produce influence. You can count on it!

When your child decides to rebel against what he has been taught remember the promise, "...when he is old, he will not depart from it." During the trial period, hold steady. The testing is bound to come because

> *I think the Bible mentions a rod because our hands are to bless, not to strike.*

even the best kids rebel. The truth is every sovereign person must be liberated at some point of maturity to make their own choices. When we choose, it must be because we believe in the choice, not because it's imposed on us. As the saying goes, a man convinced against his will is not convinced at all. Individually we all must determine the right way. We must all have the freedom to make our own choices. It's part of growing up. Each young person is given the responsibility to determine in their heart whether or not they want mom and dad's value system. Parents, God is faithful and His Word certain. Kids will come back to their training.

Let's talk more about the rod in relation to child rearing. Why does the Bible mention a rod and not something else? I think the Bible mentions a rod because our hands are to bless, not to strike. A grown man's hand can injure a child. It's much safer and more effective to use a rod. A rod should be big enough to hurt but small enough to break if you hit too hard. By the way, I'm not talking about a rod that's an inch thick and five feet long. That's child abuse!

Using the rod can provide all kinds of effective ways to discipline. First, going to get the rod itself allows you time to cool off. By the time you get back to your child you're not still livid and ready to commit murder. Going to get the stick gives you time to think and then correct them with more rationality.

When I stared using the stick on my kids, *it trained me* not to overreact. *It trained me* not to get all upset and angry and frustrated before disciplining. *It trained me* to think things through so when my kids were disobedient or wrong, I could calmly but firmly follow through with the consequences.

Second, using the rod helps kids subconsciously transfer getting pain from the parent to getting pain from the rod. Kids need to know the difference. They need to know "I'm getting the rod because I deserve it, not because my parents like hitting me." That's important because they need to accept the consequences of poor choices. The stick provides a way for them to focus on their own behavior, not the parent who is giving the discipline. They need to accept the rod as a just and fair use of discipline. I used to say to my kids, "Someday you are going to grow up and want to be something. The discipline I'm giving you right now is helping you later to discipline yourself, take responsibility, and succeed."

Let's look at Proverbs 22:15 again. "The rod of correction…" Notice, the verse does not say "the rod of punishment." It does not say "the rod of spanking" or "the rod of the father's whim." It says, "rod of correction" on purpose. You are correcting a wrong behavior, not satisfying your anger. You are correcting a wrong attitude. You are correcting disobedience. You are correcting insubordination. You are not "punishing" to release your frustration. You are "correcting" for the benefit of the child.

Consistency is huge. Here's what happens when you don't correct when you say you will: you train your child to obey only when you've told him five times, raised your voice, and your face is turning red in fury. You're teaching your child you don't have control. You're teaching him you don't mean what you say. You're teaching your child you're not a person of your word. You're teaching your child it's ok to lack integrity when it comes to certain things. You're teaching your child to do the exact same thing with his/her kids in the future.

In my old neighborhood in California there was a little boy named Manny. He was outside a lot playing in the streets around my mobile

Kenneth Teel

> How tragic to train a child that you don't follow through on your word.

home. His mom would come out every night and we would hear her call, "Manny, Manny, Manny," over and over again. One day little Manny was outside talking to me. His mother came outdoors as usual crying out his name. "Manny, Manny, come home." I said, "Aren't you going to go?" He didn't say a word. His mother kept yelling, a little louder each time. When his mothers voice reached a high pitched shrill, that's when Manny said, "***Now*** I have to go." Manny's mom had inadvertently trained her son not to respond to her until she was desperately screaming at the top of her lungs.

Where is the respect in that training?

Is that how you want things to go in your home? I don't think so. How do you prevent it from happening? Tell your child only once, not a hundred times. You tell them once clearly, firmly, "if you don't stop, I will give you a correction." If that's ignored, then you get up, go to the rod, walk back and use it with strength! It might raise a little welt on a bare leg, but the welt does not cause permanent damage and goes away quickly. The point is, the correction must hurt and also get your message across that you mean what you say **the first time**.

How tragic to train a child that you don't follow through on your word. You may say something like, "I'm not telling you again," then you tell him 50 more times. You've trained him he can wait until he's ready to obey. You've trained him he can control you because he's not responding to your wishes. You've trained him you your word is worth about as much as the air you used to speak it.

The rod actually helps parents because they can be

much more deliberate about discipline. Parents should give corrections because the child needs it, not because they're annoyed. My dad used to be very inconsistent with discipline. If he was in a good mood, he would let the most serious infractions go. If he was cranky, his discipline would be severe for practically nothing. Not good. The 'punishment' should fit the crime. My dad's discipline would leave us kids confused and resentful. Don't let emotions rule your discipline. Correct your children because they need it. Be consistent. It will pay off.

You may say, well, I don't believe in corporal punishment! Well, the Bible does - and trust me - as I said before, the Bible turns out to be right every time.

A woman approached me one day after I was teaching on child discipline and said, "I totally disagree with your teaching about using the rod." I said "Ma'am, if I didn't use the rod on my kids, they would be running all over me and out of control because I don't yell at them, I don't use my hand to strike them, and they laugh at my 'time outs.' What would you do if you had kids but you didn't yell at them, didn't' strike them with your hand, and didn't resort to verbal abuse?"

I remember times when we took our kids to dinner and forgot to bring the stick. I found it almost impossible to get them to mind when they knew I wasn't going to yell, I wasn't going to get angry, and I wasn't going to hit them with my hand. I tried talking, explaining, giving more chances, being patient, and they ignored me!

What did I have left?

Let's see, I told them they were going to get corrected when they got home – didn't work. I threatened them with going home without dinner – wasn't practical. I told them I would hang them up by their toes – didn't believe me. I tried to intimidate them by altering my voice to the lowest bass I could muster – backfired. There they were, wound up in the midst of stretching the boundaries to the limit with an "I don't

> *To discipline consistently requires self discipline!*

care," attitude. Guess what? I began taking the rod out to dinner! For their sakes I wouldn't give them discipline in front of others but would take them outside behind the car. Sometimes, the only thing that will work is the rod of correction. Don't forget to take it with you!

Proverbs 29:15 says, "The rod of correction imparts wisdom, but a child left to himself disgraces his mother." If you want to impart wisdom to your kids, use the rod. Talking isn't enough. Proverbs 23:13,14 says, "Do not withhold discipline from a child; if you punish him with the rod, he will not die. Punish him with the rod and save his soul from death." Refusing to stop children from being disrespectful, disruptive, disobedient, or not taking time to explain why they're is wrong is like pouring battery acid on a wound. They'll definitely grow up with a toxic attitude on steroids!

Again, Proverbs 13:24 says, "He who spares the rod hates his son, but he who loves him is careful to discipline him." That is a pretty aggressive statement. If you don't care enough to confront and discipline, then you **hate** your child and don't give a flip about his future.

Here's the problem for parents: It's not easy to discipline. Mom's will often cry out to daddy, "Don't spank him so hard!" Dad's fall short because they're not consistent. To discipline consistently requires self discipline!

It's difficult when you come home from a long day and you're tired and don't feel like talking about anything deeper than what's for dinner, to take time out to correct a child.

If kids are instructed not to do something and they

do it anyway, parents **must** confront them right then. After kids finish crying, they need an explanation and love afterward in the form of a hug and reassurance. That takes time and we're all busy and may be tired. It's not easy.

Consistent discipline will pay off.

When my older son was serving full time in the Air Force, he called me one day and said, "Dad, thank you so much for disciplining me and training me how to respect authority. There are so many guys in here that don't make it in the military because they've never been trained to take an order. These guys are failing, dropping out, and getting into trouble because they don't know how to handle criticism and don't have enough humility to take an order."

THE 6th KEY TO SUCCESS MOTIVATION:

Give kids good, positive, and measured discipline.

It's a good thing to value your self but that isn't pride.

CHAPTER 7

CONFRONTING PRIDE - CRITICAL IN MOTIVATING KIDS

Pride? What's wrong with it?

It hurts us, hinders us, and lies to us. It makes us look like fools. Yet we persist in holding on to it. We're told to humble ourselves, sit in a lower seat, and be modest. What do we do instead? We boast, promote ourselves, and knock the other guy down that's ahead of us.

Pride is incredibly pernicious. It has afflicted mankind throughout history. The great king Solomon uttered this famous saying in the book of Ecclesiastes: "Vanity, vanity, all is vanity." Ecclesiastes 1:2 (KJV)

Someone once said there is a 'good' kind of pride. I don't think so. What they mean is it's a good thing to give your self credit for a job well done. That's not pride, it's telling the truth.

In contrast, pride leads us to lie, delude, and deceive ourselves by ignoring the facts. It exaggerates our own personal achievements and minimizes others.

It's a good thing to value your self but that isn't pride.

Robert Schuller once aptly stated, "It's not a sin to love what God loves." It's not pride to love ourselves or acknowledge a job well done. Pride is when we think we can do no wrong. Pride is when we think everyone around us is an idiot. Pride is when we listen only to ourselves and no one else.

Pride is no respecter of age, race, economic status, gender, or rank. There are people who have very little outwardly, yet exhibit extreme pride. Some live in lower income housing, drive beat up cars, wear ghetto clothing, have little education, suffer from either morbid obesity or a famine figure, yet they bristle with arrogance. They have a condescending, judgmental attitude toward everyone and everything in their world.

At the other end of the spectrum, millionaires can fall to the same attitudes. They isolate themselves and justify it because they've succeeded more than others and on that basis are superior.

Then again, there are those who have an abundance of wealth but aren't impressed with themselves in the least. They're intelligent, financially well to do, hold prestigious positions in their community, train at the gym, yet live in true humility. There are also the poor who have made humility a way of life.

Humility is the key to knowledge, truth and the abundant life.

In contrast, pride deceives.

Pride causes us to believe that "I" am at the center of the universe." It alters reality and leads us to think "I'm better." It leads us to embrace an elitist attitude and blows a smoke screen to hide the truth about our own failures.

> *Humility is the key to knowledge, truth and the abundant life.*

Pride is something to recognize and deal with in ourselves before we can help our kids deal with it. There's a difference I've said, between doing a good job and being happy about it, versus having a haughty attitude that says "I'm better than everyone else." Pride distorts because it blinds us from seeing the facts.

James 4:6 says, "…God opposes the proud but gives grace to the humble."

Pride disables, prevaricates, and tells us to defend ourselves. It urges us to brag, because if we don't, no one will notice us. Pride is at the core of contention in every relationship. "Pride only breeds quarrels, but wisdom is found in those who take advice." Proverbs 13:10

Do you want grace from God instead of opposition from God? Grace means undeserved favor, but it also means being given the power to do what's right. Do you want the power to do what's right? What you need is grace. If you're prideful, you're not getting the grace you need to live successfully. Instead you're fighting God at every turn.

"In his arrogance the wicked man hunts down the weak who are caught in the schemes he devises. He boasts of the cravings of his heart; he blesses the greedy and reviles the Lord. In his pride the wicked does not seek him; in all his thoughts there is no room for God….he is haughty and your laws are far from him; he sneers at all his enemies. He says to himself, "nothing will shake me; I'll always be happy and never have trouble. His mouth is full of curses and lies and threats; trouble and evil are under his tongue." Psalm 10:2-7 That's a pretty miserable description of pride isn't it? This scripture unfolds 12 characteristics of a prideful man:

#1 ***The prideful man is an arrogant bully who's looking for a fight.*** ("In his arrogance the wicked man hunts down the weak who are caught in the schemes he devises.")

#2 ***The prideful man is a braggart who is not ashamed to talk*** *about his exploits which satisfy only himself* ("...he boasts of the cravings of his heart...")

#3 ***The prideful man does not seek God.*** ("In his pride, the wicked does not seek him;...")

#4 ***His values are completely skewed taking his place with the greedy, giving them approval, all the while spurning the Lord and everything good.*** ("...he blesses the greedy and reviles the Lord.")

#5 ***The prideful person is a lawless person who pushes God out of his thoughts.*** ("...in all his thoughts there is no room for God... he is haughty and your laws are far from him.")

#6 ***The prideful of heart exhibit a bad attitude toward anyone who disagrees with him."*** ("...he sneers at all his enemies.")

#7 ***The prideful man is over confident.*** ("He says to himself, 'nothing will ever shake me; I'll always be happy and never have any trouble.") What planet is this man living on? Trouble is a part of life.

#8 ***The prideful man does not bless others but curses them instead.*** ("His mouth is full of curses...")

#9 ***The prideful man is a liar.*** ("His mouth is full of...lies...")

#10 ***The prideful man is a violent man.*** ("His mouth is full of... threats...")

#11 ***The prideful man is a trouble maker.*** (..."trouble...is under his tongue.")

#12 ***His tongue is poison.*** ("...evil is under his tongue.")

Do you see why pride is so incredibly evil? It's absolutely essential in raising kids not to underestimate this vicious enemy. It's critical for parents to spot pride and confront it early.

Kid's make a lot of prideful statements that should be corrected, albeit with patience, gentleness, and wisdom.

It's critical for parents to spot pride and confront it early.

When pride isn't confronted early, it's power can easily sweep kids into grave delusion, pushing success further and further away from their grasp. But humility isn't imparted until we have it ourselves.

When I was pastoring in Southern California, a cherished woman in our congregation came to me one day and said, "Pastor, I've really tried to take an objective look at myself but I just can't see that I have any faults. As you can imagine, it was difficult to talk to her about anything because she was 'perfect.' Her view was superior pertaining to every subject. She had a higher spirituality, more knowledge, and in her eyes, was without fault! That's pride at its worse!

As I reflect on this now, I'm sure the Lord has since changed this well meaning saint. I can't imagine the Lord allowing anyone to stay in that condition. She made these remarks to me when I was a young pastor. She said it so convincingly that I almost believed her. Pride had completely taken her and it was exacting a great price in her personality. She had inadvertently adopted an elitist attitude pushing everyone away from her.

Kids have pride too.

How should parents deal with it? Well, the same way you would deal with any other problem. YOU CONFRONT IT! You're an adult. You know when a child is being prideful. Point it out to them with kindness. Pray for them. Don't let them get away with saying and doing prideful things.

One Sunday while I was teaching 4th, 5th, and 6th graders at church, one of the 6th grade boys - I'll call him "Billy" -

began picking on a younger boy in the 5th grade - I'll call him "Bobby." This 6th grader was unusually big for his age and would not listen to me telling him repeatedly to stop bothering the younger student. Finally I said, "I understand why you're not listening to me. You think what you are doing is more important than what I'm doing." By the way, I didn't say this to the student, but that's pride! Then I said, "I challenge you to an arm wrestle." "If I win, then you agree to stop picking on Bobby, O.K?" "Sure," He said, "Oh, but I can beat you!" No problem." Pride again!

Why did I create this challenge? He was showing no respect and my words weren't enough to restrain his rudeness!

I invited him up front and we went to the floor. The other kids gathered around as loud cheering began. I think the kids were on the boy's side. I held his arm until his face turned red and said, "Have you started yet?" He tried all the harder. He squirmed and writhed on the floor trying with all his might to beat me. At the end, I prevailed and said, "Now, will you stop picking on Bobby?" He went back to his seat silently and there were no more problems that day.

I created that challenge on purpose to give this disruptive bully a wake up call and it worked! He thought he didn't have to listen. He thought he was strong enough to promote his agenda without resistance. He wanted to pick on Bobby and thought the teacher was too afraid to stop him. He thought the freedom to do whatever he wanted trumped what I was doing.

"Billy" was prideful. He was picking on the smaller boy because perhaps he got away with it in the past. He did not respond to my patient admonitions to stop, so I realized he needed more. He imagined he was "Rambo." In my humble opinion challenging him was the most effective teaching tool at the time. If he wasn't exhibiting pride, what was he exhibiting? Why did he say, "Oh, I can beat you," a clearly ridiculous proposition? **Pride.** (I'm not a wimp, by the way).

The very next week the same scenario began with "Billy" picking on "Bobby." I said to "Billy," "Don't you remember last week when I beat you arm wrestling?" He said, "Oh, you didn't beat me, I beat you." So I said, "You don't remember? Come up front for another round." I effortlessly beat him again. He was quiet the rest of the class. Why did he say he'd beaten me when he hadn't? **Pride.**

Sometimes we need to catch kids in the lies they are telling themselves and figure out a way to not just tell them, but to demonstrate to them how foolish they've been by pushing out their chest and challenging all-comers.

The Bible says, "...Knowledge puffs up, but love builds up. The man who thinks he knows something does not yet know as he ought to know." I Corinthians 8:1,2 I used to wonder about the meaning of that verse. After many humbling events in my life and having to back down and admit I was wrong on so many occasions, I figured this verse out. It means anyone who thinks they are smarter than God, knows nothing!

Why is it that we "know nothing?" Let's explore this for a moment because it's critical in teaching kids humility. Take the human body for example. Do you think you know something about the human body? If you're a doctor, you know more than the average person, but collectively all the doctors on planet earth know **less** about the human body than there is *to* know.

There are approximately one hundred trillion cells in the human body. Each cell contains approximately 3 billion bits of information. Now, tell me, how is it that anyone can know the human body when there's almost an infinite number of chemical reactions, brain waves, blood cells, and processes all happening simultaneously with billions of combinations of amino acids and proteins interacting with one another at the same time?

The answer is we don't know. As a matter of fact, we don't know much about anything!

Take the simplest of objects for instance, like a paper clip. You may think you know a lot about the paper clip and you probably do, but you may know less about it than you think. Where was it manufactured? Where did the metal originate? What is the manufacturer's name? What is the name of the person who pushed the button to twist it into shape in the factory? Who sold it to the retailer where you bought it? Who invented the paper clip? What is the paper clips' weight? How many uses are there for the paper clip? And on and on it goes.

You might say, "I don't want to know any more about a paper clip than I already know." Well, I don't either. All we really need to know is where to buy them. The point is this is a lesson in humility we need to pass on to our kids. We know incredibly *less* about life than we *think* we know.

I've been in Christian ministry for many years. The Bible has been my main text and study book over all others. I have spent much time studying the Bible everyday for many years, preparing teachings, researching sermons, and writing Bible studies. I know quite a bit about the Bible. Yet, I can unequivocally say, "I know almost infinitely less about the Bible than there is to know, even though I may be more knowledgeable than the average person."

So it's good to get the right perspective. I once preached a sermon on "knowing the Word". I said, "I hear people glibly say all the time they *know* the word of God. That's like saying you know every word in the Webster's New

> *It's critical we teach our kids humility by our own example.*

International College Dictionary that's about ten inches thick!" All of us are very limited, so let's admit it so we can move forward.

It's critical we teach our kids humility by our own example. If kids keep hanging on to the foolish pride of childhood, they will hit a block wall that will stop them from being all they can be.

"Let another praise you, and not your own mouth; someone else, and not your own lips." Proverbs 27:2 I used to quote this verse to my kids when they would brag about themselves. I would remind them, "You aren't the best in the world, and even if you were, you need to recognize your ability is a *gift* and be humbly grateful for it.

Why do muscle builders' strut in front of a mirror? Could it be pride? Why do we exaggerate when telling a story? Could that be pride? Why do we hide so many of our own weaknesses? Is it Pride? Why do we get in arguments with people over trivial stuff? Pride again? Do we not do these things because we don't want to be exposed as a phony, embarrassed for not knowing the answer, or look smaller or weaker than someone else?

Pride was the original sin of Satan. His heavenly name was "Lucifer," which means 'light bearer.' You don't want to be like Satan do you?

He was a perfectly created heavenly being. He was beautiful, wise, the chief musician, and a leader of the angelic host. He lived in the all glorious, radiant, almighty presence of God! Yet his pride caused him to fall from his position and become man's nemesis for all time. He looked to himself instead of God. He exalted himself and attempted a take over of God's throne, like that was ever going to happen. There is only one God and He is God! God tells us to praise Him not because He is on a divine ego trip but because He *is* worthy. The truth is, He made everything, knows everything, is all-powerful, infinite, and yet a personal God. Why shouldn't we praise Him?

Pride was also the original sin of Adam and Eve. (It wasn't eating an apple.)

This is dangerous to all of us. Take time to make clear to kids how they need to be aware of pride's insidious nature and it's blinding effects on our souls.

Pride is the other side of the self esteem coin. If you were given a gift, like $100,000, would you brag about it and take credit for earning it? Honesty would say,' "this was given to me." There is a kind of humbling that goes along with that utterance! If it's God who gives us everything we have, including our minds, bodies, and abilities, then why do we boast as if we did something to produce them?

The children of Israel were **given** the land of promise. Did they deserve it? No! They of all people deserved it least! They complained, doubted, sinned against God and fought with Moses. There is no way the Israelites could take credit for that great accomplishment. God **gave** them the Land of Canaan, period. A gift precludes bragging.

Teaching kids humility is showing them that everything they have is a gift from God. It's true we must work, cooperate, learn, and be responsible, but we could do all of those things and still not have the blessings unless God released them to us.

To further illustrate, let's say a father with two sixteen year old sons informs them one day he wants to give each of them a car. "I want to give each of you a car but there is going to be a trial period," he says. "If you come home when I ask, don't get any tickets, drive safely with no accidents, and maintain your car, I will give you the car at the end of six months.

During the trial period, the first son always came

Teaching kids humility is showing them that everything they have is a gift from God.

home on time. He polished the car, didn't get tickets, and listened when his dad gave special instructions.

The second son consistently came home late, didn't maintain the car, and left it unwashed. He got several tickets besides driving recklessly. At the end of six months, the first son was given his car but the second son was not.

Question? Why did the first son get the car?

We could say the father gave it because the son did what the father asked him. The son did his part, that's important, but the point is if the father had not ***wanted*** to give the car, it wouldn't have mattered what either of the sons did. The gift was based on the father's heart of generosity, performance was secondary.

This illustrates our relationship with God. Using our gifts encompasses the realization that without the gifts, there would be no achievement.

Who gave us our minds? Who gave you our bodies, our talents? Who gave us the time to use them? Who brings others into our lives to bless us? If the Lord didn't want to ***give*** these things, we wouldn't have them! "Humility and the fear of the Lord bring wealth and honor and life." Proverbs 22:4

Teaching humility to kids isn't done in a vacuum. A classroom is not the best place to learn it. It's better "caught" than "taught" through parents daily modeling humility before their kids.

I want to challenge you today. Be humble in front of your children and humble in private. Be humble on your job, in your marriage and as a dad or mom. The result? Your kids will most definitely catch on to succeeding!

THE 7th KEY
TO SUCCESS MOTIVATION:

Take on humility and teach it to your children.

> *A powerful key in relating to kids is listening to them.*

CHAPTER 8

WHAT ABOUT KID'S OPINIONS, HOW MUCH DO THEY COUNT?

Kids opinions *are* important, even though grown-ups may not think so.

Kids are often wrong – we all know that – why not cut them some slack and acknowledge their opinions and respect what they think? If necessary, **afterwards** you can correct their facts or perspective. The popular T.V. show "Are You Smarter Than a 5th Grader?" has shown that kids can be pretty sharp!

A powerful key in relating to kids is listening to them. That's a good way to love them. I've noticed that kids gravitate toward me. Why? I listen to them. It's not complicated. How can kids relate to you if you never give them the time of day?

Kid's have opinions like everyone else. Parents ought not let their own pride or impatience cut kids off before they've had a chance to share their hearts. Parents aren't always right but they can easily project that idea onto kids. When parents feel over confident they can easily minimize what kids say or simply turn them off.

I've noticed that kids aren't used to being listened to - so when they are - it delights them no end. When my grandson Rylind was five years old, he hardly ever got his facts straight. Of course! He was only five years old! As I would listen to him, nod, and say, "uh ha," his little eyes would light up and his face beam with the show of respect and acceptance. Later, when the time was right, I would take time to gently straighten out flaws in his facts and logic. That's loving him and motivating him at the same time. I'm not putting the kibosh on everything that comes out of his mouth. Who wouldn't feel rejected if that were done to them?

Most kids love to talk. Why not take the opportunity to help them develop their thinking skills by letting them talk? I know that takes more than a little patience! Playing games like monopoly, checkers, hangman, or a variety of other games is a good way to let them think for themselves while providing a positive platform from which to show them a better way when they mess up.

There's always an exception to the rule and my daughter Ali did not fit the 'kids loving to talk rule.' When I would take her to eighth grade everyday, I would try to make conversation with her as we drove over the curvy, small mountain pass toward her school. The ride to school lasted about 20 minutes so instead of sitting in silence - which would've happened if I'd said nothing - I would ask her questions in an attempt to get her to talk. I quickly learned questions requiring more than a "yes" or "no" or one word response wasn't going to work. I would ask her, "How do you like your teachers?" She would mumble, "Fine." "Are you making friends?" A muffled "Yes," came her half-hearted response. It took a lot of effort to figure out ways to get her to open up but I didn't give up and my persistence paid off! She has grown into a very warm, kind, and compassionate wife and mom.

> *I would rather patiently listen to something wrong or foolish than to dismiss kids before they've really had a chance to fully express themselves.*

The only way we're really going to find out what kids are thinking is to ask them, then **listen** without judging as they talk.

Listening is a good beginning.

You might imagine kids have straight thinking. Go ahead and let them talk and you'll quickly find out that most of the time they're blowing smoke! We all know kids can say whacky stuff, yet if they fear telling you what they think because you treat them with disrespect, impatience, or minimize their ideas, they won't venture to be honest with you and you'll loose the opportunity to really get to know them or genuinely help them. Closing your ears or half listening sacrifices valuable information about them you could use to help them grow!

I would rather patiently listen to something wrong or foolish than to dismiss kids before they've really had a chance to fully express themselves. If I do that, kids will pretend when they're around me and tell me what they think I want to hear. Not good.

By dismissing a conversation too soon, you lose the chance to connect with kids. To develop rapport with them or actually agree with them, you have to be humble and honest enough to share your feelings with them as they share their feelings with you.

Kids don't mind being wrong if they're not put down for it! I think it would be good to remind ourselves often that we were all kids once and didn't know what we were talking about half the time either! Give grace to the younger generation and they will let you patiently guide them to the truth.

One day I was teaching my son Rob about the pitfalls of rock music. He argued with me all night about it. We would go back and forth, debating whether it was a good or bad thing. I always let him express his opinion but would try to go deeper in showing him the problem behind the problem. Being a music teacher, I naturally would talk a little more about the technical aspects. I taught him the three aspects of music: melody, harmony, and rhythm. I would say, "When all you hear is the beat, the music is missing two elements and tends to increase your heart rate and bombard your lower nature. When you can't understand the words, you don't know what message the song is giving, and when there is an indistinguishable melody, the music tends to cause tension, not peace.

This discussion seemed to go on for weeks. One day I bought him a CD and listened to it with him as we were taking a trip in the car. He would also listen to the music on his Walkman.

After listening for a while, he said, "Dad, this music isn't good." I said, "Oh? Why?" I responded further, "I can't tell. It seems pretty mellow to me." He handed the earphones to me and I listened to the song with a very nice melody, "Basketball, I wanna play basketball." What we could not hear from the car speakers was the guy whispering under his breath, "Shoot the pill." We could only hear that with the earphones on. Tricky! The message could not be heard by parents. It was a secret message only for the kids. Rob willingly shared this with me because he was not fearful of what I might say to him. He knew

The Bible is such a great book because it's always right!

what was right, he simply needed the encouragement to openly acknowledge it.

The Bible is such a great book because it's always right! If we know what the Bible says about a variety subjects, then we're better prepared to make sure of what we're talking about. When kids reflect on how they think compared to what the Bible says, it becomes clear to them very quickly how inadequate their judgment is.

It's wise to teach kids not to buy into to just 'anyone's' opinions. It's also wise to teach kids to check out their own opinions before they loudly and confidently spew foolishness all over the room and have to endure the humiliation of being wrong, eating their words, or being corrected by someone publicly.

There are few things I hate more than demonstrating my ignorance. If you've lived long enough, you know what it's like to be wrong. Being wrong once in a while is just a fact of life and that's ok. No one is right all the time but I've learned through sheer embarrassment, whenever I think everyone else is wrong and I'm right in a situation, it's better to move forward cautiously with my thoughts and opinions than to make a fool of myself. It's great to be confident but it's far superior to make sure I know what I'm talking about before I open my mouth. Why not use wisdom and be a little slower to speak?

I think it's a good thing for everyone to develop the habit of checking his or her facts before making a judgment. This is incredibly important because kids tend to believe whatever they hear. Persons who check out their facts and get them straight are considered wise. Feelings are very important but feelings rarely have anything to do with facts. We can all feel good or bad about a lot of things, but the feelings may or may not have anything to do with truth or reality.

Teaching kids about getting their facts straights is huge. It's very easy to misinterpret a person's facial expression, tone of voice, or body language and jump to wrong conclusions without the facts. Making evaluations from "dirty looks" leads to hurt feelings, gossip, tension, or anger.

One day the drummer on our worship team came to me and said, "I'm quitting." I said, "Oh, Why?" He said, "Because Grandma Betty gives me dirty looks while I'm playing the drums and I'm tired of it!" "If people don't want me up there drumming, then forget it, I'll just go somewhere else." I said, "Well, I don't think you really know what grandma Betty is thinking." He said, "Oh yes I do, I know by her face," I replied, "Well, I've seen her face for many years and must humbly admit I used to think she was against me too. I thought she disapproved of my preaching. However, by watching her long enough, I realized that's how she looks all the time!"

Sure. When it came to musical styles, Grandma Betty was from the old school and probably didn't appreciate the drums as much in worship as everyone else, but her facial expressions were the result of gravity, stress, and the pressures of life, not her displeasure with the drummer.

I've often said, "If you can't prove something in a court of law, then you can't be sure you're right, even when the situation shouts at 50 decibels that you are right and the other person wrong. Unless you have concrete evidence, you don't really know another person's thoughts or the reasons behind his or her actions. I know that sounds a bit extreme, but it's true. Unless you know for certain - with facts to back it up - you are standing only on hearsay, gossip, or assumptions, not truth.

I'll admit I've also been very sensitive people's facial

> *Unless you have concrete evidence, you don't really know another person's thoughts or the reasons behind his or her actions.*

expressions. I've been prone to read something negative into people's faces instead of something positive. It's for this very reasons I've stopped looking at other people while I'm driving. I'm much more at peace now that I ignore what used to look to me like an angry face or disapproving gesture. In reality, those looks had nothing to do with me. Perhaps those other drivers were having a bad day or their faces in a relaxed position just happened to look like Jack the Ripper, or maybe they were simply expelling gas. I don't look at other drivers anymore and I'm much more at rest.

Reserving judgment against others is huge in developing healthy relationships. We are so quick to judge another person's motives, or what they're thinking, or feeling, or why they act in certain ways. In reality, we don't know any of these things. We don't know what someone is thinking until we ask them or they volunteer it.

The book of Proverbs - the wisdom book of the Bible says – it's wise to listen to both sides before making a judgment.

When I first started out in ministry and was doing marital counseling, I would listen to one side of a troubled relationship and find myself sympathizing and siding with that person and thinking, "They're spouse is so wrong!" What they told me about the other person seemed so convincing and unfair. I thought, "How immature of that other person!" However, when I heard the other side, I was shocked to discover the other person had just as convincing a story as the first!

Kids are human beings just like grown-ups. Give them

> *Reserving judgment against others is huge in developing healthy relationships.*

the same value you give everyone else. Don't cut them off, disregard their opinions and ridicule their ideas. Even when wrong - which may be often - their feelings about what they think are valid. What they think is right and true to them until they're shown a better way.

Kids are validated and grow into healthy and successful adults when they're allowed to talk and allowed to be wrong!

THE 8th KEY TO SUCCESS MOTIVATION:

Affirm children's ideas.

Kids need freedom appropriate to their age, maturity level, and their track record with handling past responsibilities.

CHAPTER 9

HOW MUCH FREEDOM, WHEN?

What do you say to kids when they're pressuring you for more freedom?

I've noticed two extremes in parenting. I've seen kids lives ruined because parents weren't able to let go and I've seen kids ruined because parents were in "la la land" with no clue as to what their own kids were doing under their own roof.

Is there such a thing as being too strict? Yes. Is there such a thing as being too permissive? Yes. Is there is a danger of going to one extreme or the other? Of course. What can you do to achieve a balance?

I want to say something at the beginning of this chapter that may rub you the wrong way but it's a strong personal belief. After being a dad, teacher, minister, and grandpa for many years, I think it's better for parents to err on the side of giving too much freedom to their kids than to turn their home into a military camp that runs like a prison.

Let me explain.

Kids want and need freedom. I don't think there's any debate about that. The question is: when should they get *more* freedom? Kids need freedom appropriate to their age, maturity level, and their track record with handling past responsibilities. Without freedom kids will not adjust well, more likely rebel, and not be able to function responsibly later. Without the right amount of freedom, kids may even develop disorders that put them at risk and at a clear disadvantage with their peers. On the other hand, too much freedom is just as harmful.

Let me share with you a true story about too much freedom. While I was living in Southern California, Chris age 14, was a good friend of my son Rob. They attended the same school and hung out together all the time. He was always over at our house, raiding the refrigerator, playing video games, and otherwise pushing my annoyance level to the limit. One day Chris called me from school crying. He said, "My parents left for vacation to Missouri. They said I could go to my uncle's house but I can't go back. Last night there was an orgy and drug party at his house and I just can't go back there again." I responded, "You mean your parents left you home alone for three weeks?" "Oh, they said I could go to my uncle's if I wanted, but I just can't do it. Can I come and stay with you?" I began bristling with anger on the inside. What were Chris's parents thinking? I couldn't believe they left Chris home alone. That was an incredibly irresponsible and thoughtless things to do. Talk about neglect and abuse! What they did was like handing a loaded gun to a child and telling him to play with it. Here was Chris left alone at 14 years of age with the freedom to do literally *anything* he wanted.

I told Chris he could stay over our house and called his parents to tell them I would keep Chris.

Wouldn't you agree Chris's parents were making a totally bad and inappropriate decision for their son, not to mention selfish?! Left alone in this culture at age 14? What kind of destructive forces were unleashed on Chris in his parent's absence? He was exposed to pornography, sex, drugs, alcohol, criminal activity, and violence. It's a wonder his parents came home to a house that was still standing. Parents you've got a huge problem if you go away for a week-or-two vacation and leave your 14 year old son or daughter to fend for themselves. By the way, the scenario I've described happens far more often than you want to know.

Parents, do you realize what you are doing when you allow stuff like that? I know it sounds like I'm beating up on parents right now - but in case you haven't noticed - kids have sexual issues. Why throw gasoline on the fire of their already out-of- control struggles? What parents are saying when they leave big gaps of unexplained time expenditures in their kids schedules is: "Hey, while we're away, go ahead and party, it's o.k. we did. Just be safe and use condoms and don't go out if you drink. Parents, what are you thinking?

I was teaching piano to three bright, beautiful girls in a wealthy home in southern California a few years ago. All three girls seemed pretty well-adjusted and making modest progress on the piano. The middle daughter seemed particularly troubled and rebellious.

Over the course of time the middle daughter hooked up with a boy friend she started bringing home on a regular basis. The two of them would go prancing upstairs to the girl's bedroom and close the door. All the while the parents were down in the kitchen with music on, drinking, entertaining, or watching T.V.

What was going on in her parent's minds?

Did they really think their daughter and her boyfriend were doing homework? Maybe. But the unspoken message handed to the girl by her parents was, "You can do anything you want because no one is watching." That kind of "freedom" is damaging. That kind of "freedom" needs to be confronted. Somebody in that girl's life needed to step up to the plate and take the "guff" for being a "narrow minded," "puritanical," and "overprotective" adult and say "no," you can't go into the bedroom alone and close the door!"

I believe these parents loved their daughters. I believe they wanted the best for them. These parents were intelligent, made a six-figured income, and were socially mobile. They gave everything you can imagine to their girls - except discretion.

Tragically like so many others, these parents didn't know how to say "no" when "no" was begging to be said. These parents were caught up with their own friends, social life, and recreation. They didn't know how to identify their daughter's rebellion nor did they want to bother helping her make good decisions.

Another example of good people who needed help is Paula's parents, the other side of the coin to the parental "it's all good" philosophy.

Paula's parents loved her but didn't know how to let her grow up. When she turned 14, they wouldn't allow her to go out with friends, even in groups. There was always a reason she couldn't do something. Her parents even had difficulty letting her become involved at church. I don't know the whole story because I didn't live in that home, but this girl began to rise up against her parents. Every chance she got she rebelled. Resentment and anger between her and her parents grew to a higher and higher level until tension was nearly always visible between them. She grew up in a wonderful Christian home with parents who had unintentionally laid the groundwork for her to move in with her boyfriend at age 19. This kind of scenario tragically is not the exception but the rule.

> *Tragically like so many others, these parents didn't know how to say "no" when "no" was begging to be said.*

I think parents need to "keep in touch" with their kids, knowing where they are mentally, emotionally, and spiritually, not to speak of knowing where they are geographically! However, I also think parents need to wake up and realize how they are cheating their kids out of growing up if they don't give them freedom!

Parents who take on the responsibility of making **all** decisions for their kids, unwittingly steal from them the chance to learn how to make and take responsibility for their own decisions.

How do you determine the right amount of freedom to give at what age?

Here's a rule of thumb: if a child has obeyed in the past, taken responsibility given to them, listened, stayed within the boundaries given to them at each stage of their development, then they are ready for more freedom. If they mess up with more freedom, then that new freedom should be put on hold for a while until they are ready.

My son used to say, "Dad, how come you won't let me go out?" "You don't trust me!" I would always reply, "You're right son, I don't trust you because I don't trust human nature. I don't trust myself when I'm given too much freedom and no one is watching." I would continue, "You need accountability with your freedom and that's what I'm here for. I will admit you do need freedom, but with restraints and with an understanding between us. When you can prove yourself in smaller things, you will earn the right to gain additional privileges."

That's being reasonable, fair, and smart.

I think anything less is a "pretend adult/child relationship" where the child is running the show or the parent is not paying attention to their job, or the parent is overreacting to any attempt on the child's part to grow up and their need to experience "freedom within limits."

My kid's friends used to play with matches. One day Raymond, a friend of my son, managed to burn down a mobile home where we lived.

As I result of that mishap, I started telling my son, "Son, if I give you permission to go out into the field and you play with matches without me knowing, God's blessing will lift from your life. God's presence will never leave you, but His blessing will and you never want God's blessing to be gone from you." That may seem a bit heavy handed, but it's the truth and it gave my kids something to think about. By the way, my kids never did play with matches.

Here is a good motto for parents: **Freedom within limits at the right time!**

I didn't allow any of my kids to have their own vehicle until they were 18. Call me backwards. Call me 'out of it.' Call me cruel. In my view, vehicles give a teenager an almost infinite amount of freedom they're not ready for. They can jump in a car and be a 100 miles a way in just a couple of hours. They can be alone with whomever they wish in a car. They can drive like a maniac without anyone knowing until a cop stops them or someone finds them crashed at the bottom of a gorge. That kind of parenting style could mean the signing of your child's death warrant.

The trick is extending your child's latitude of freedom in measured increments. Kids need additional responsibility, trust, and freedom as they grow. What damages them is either extreme of carte blanche privileges without accountability or prison camp enslavement. Balance is the key. A home military camp is a training ground for disaster waiting to happen. On the other hand, freedom without question is a recipe for really bad consequences as well.

Freedom comes from the inner strength to say "no" to oneself and that only happens after we've learned self control. We live in a human body with lots of desires and cravings. We can only be free from those desires and cravings when we discover the power within to set limits. Knowing how weak we really are is a good thing because it causes us to turn from ourselves to God. It raises to the surface our dependence on a power greater than ourselves.

Kids are in the early stages of getting acquainted with just how weak their resolve is in the face of their appetites and desires. They desperately need wise adults and biblical principles to guide them. Millions of people pick up addictions they can't break because they were given too much freedom growing up or they were never given any real choices to make along the way. We can only get free by allowing Christ to come on the inside and break all bondages that enslave us.

Knowing how to possess the inner territory of our own souls is a critical issue. God was right when He gave us free will. As much pain, destruction, and misery it has caused on planet earth, He knew there could be no real love without freedom. There can be no discovery without it, no failure, and no success. What needs to be imparted to kids is the understanding of exactly what freedom is. What are we getting free from and what are we getting free to become?

Paul the apostle said, "Am I now trying to win the approval of men, or of God? Or am I trying to please men? If I were still trying to please men, I would not be a servant of Christ." Galatians 1:10

Paul discovered who and what he was serving. It was only then that he was truly free. Bob Dylan used to sing, "You've got to serve somebody." Teaching kids that freedom is not doing what your mind and body tell you, but doing what is right is the path to success.

THE 9th KEY TO SUCCESS MOTIVATION:

Give freedom to kids at the right time.

CHAPTER 10

Problem Solving and Motivating Kids with Seeds of Faith

It's been said that after Columbus discovered America, he was sitting around a table with some colleagues talking about it. One of his friends spoke up and said, "Well, Chris, if you hadn't discovered America, one of *us* would have."

Columbus asked for a chicken egg nearby and passed it around and challenged his friends to stand it on end. The egg went around the circle as each person tried to stand it up on end. No one at the table could do it. When it came back to Columbus, he cracked the egg and stood it up on end. Then he said, "None of you could stand the egg on end before - now only after I have shown you - are you able to do it."

There are many challenges in life like cracking that egg. There often seems to be no answer to our dilemmas and we grow discouraged and want to give up. Yet it never fails, ***after*** we discover how to solve the problem, it seems so easy!

There are thousands of people everyday who feel like quitting because they don't know how to think thoroughly, independently, or tenaciously about their problems. No one has ever taught them there ***is*** a solution to every problem!

In case you haven't noticed yet, life is a continuous series of problems to solve. How am I going to pay my bills? How am I going to get physically fit? What job am I going to find? Where should I go to school? When am I going to get married? How am I going to make it to heaven? The list goes on and on.

For kids to grow up adequately equipped to solve problems, they should be allowed very early to solve their own problems. Interfering adults don't make problems better for kids. Kids should be challenged to think for themselves. The adults in their lives don't need to fix everything for them so they won't feel any pain. Kids need to be left alone to think about how to solve their problems.

I must continually be on guard while teaching music not to give answers to student's questions too quickly. I naturally want to give answers immediately because I'm the teacher and have a passion for my students to learn. I've realized that students will have a more rewarding learning experience if I ask them more questions or ask them what they think instead of offering up the answer. If I can lead them to answers without telling them, it forces them to think the problem through on their own, and that inevitably leads to recalling the answer with more clarity. It also gives them a better understanding of music theory because they were allowed to process the reasons behind music structure.

Sure, kids do need guidance, encouragement, and help when they are confused and have questions, but they don't need to be rescued every time they stress out or cry about their problems.

> *In case you haven't noticed yet, life is a continuous series of problems to solve.*

One day I was talking to my son about faith in God and quoted the Bible passage that says, "…Everything is possible for him who believes." (Mark 9:23) I finished by saying, "Son, anything I absolutely have to do, I can do." With a great deal of self assurance he retorted, "Oh Dad, you can't pick up this mobile home!" I said, "Well, maybe I can't pick it up with my own strength, but I could surely find a way to do it if I had to!"

Kids give up easily. Don't we all! We need to be challenged not to throw in the towel the minute we hit an obstacle. If you believe in God, certainly there is nothing impossible to Him. "…with God all things are possible." Matthew 19:26 If He is on your side, then it stands to reason that there is also nothing impossible to you! "…I tell you the truth, if you have faith as small as a mustard seed, you can say to this mountain, 'Move from here to there' and it will move. Nothing will be impossible for you." Matthew 17:20

It's important we understand the meaning of the word 'seed' in this verse. The writers of the New International Version and other translations assumed Jesus was talking about the *size* of the mustard seed and so translated this verse in Matthew 17:20 "…if you have faith *as small as* a mustard seed…"

The King James Version however states, "…If ye have faith *as* a grain of mustard seed, ye shall say unto this mountain, Remove hence to yonder place; and it shall remove; and nothing shall be impossible unto you" Matthew 17:20 (KJV). Notice there is an important distinction in this verse between these two translations.

When Jesus says *"as"* a grain of mustard seed, He is speaking of the *quality* of the seed, not its *size*. He didn't say *"as small as."* That's something the translators added. It's true the mustard seed is tiny, but the point Jesus makes here refers to the *ability* of the seed to grow, in spite of its smallness at the beginning. It's about what happens to the seed that's important.

We need to get what this verse means. How many know it takes more than 'little faith' to move a mountain?! You can't do much with 'little faith' for very long. When Jesus bid Peter to walk on the water to him, Peter ended up sinking and Jesus saying, "O thou of little faith, wherefore didst thou doubt? Matthew 14:31b (KJV).

You can start off walking on water with 'little faith' but it takes more than 'little faith' to keep walking on water!

Jesus called Peter's faith "little." Why? I thought Peter was doing pretty well. No one else was getting out of the boat. He at least walked on water for a moment and I've never down that except when the water was frozen! Why did Jesus call Peter's faith little? Notice the rest of the verse. "...wherefore didst thou doubt?" Matthew 14:31b (KJV). Peter had faith, but he doubted. Isn't that what we often do? We start out in faith but can't make it through because of our unbelief.

When I was growing up in church, I was told many times by my well-meaning Sunday school teachers that all we needed as Christians was a small amount of faith - the size of a mustard seed - to move a mountain. Not true! I thought it strange that no one was ever moving any mountains in that church if all it took was a little bit of faith!

It takes great faith to move mountains! Here's what my Sunday school teacher's misunderstood. When Jesus was talking about the seed, He was talking about the "nature of the seed." The seed starts off small but grows when it's cultivated. It starts out not able to produce much but can grow big enough to cast out demons, heal the sick, raise the dead, conquer sin, and produce all kinds of supernatural miracles!

The good news of the gospel is that all of us begin with 'little faith' which makes slight accomplishments. If we will develop it, exercise it, and be patient, it can grow into 'great faith.'

Jesus spoke another parable about the seed that's important for us to look at. "Another parable put he forth unto them, saying, The kingdom of heaven is like to a grain of mustard seed, which a man took, and sowed in his field; Which indeed is the least of all seeds: but when it is grown, it is the greatest among herbs, and becomes a tree, so that the birds of the air come and lodge in the branches thereof." Matthew 13:31-32 (KJV)

This verse also talks about the power of the seed. It's talking about the remarkable possibilities in a very small seed to produce an abundance over time. What is the seed in this parable? The Bible reveals that the 'seed' is the word. Jesus in His explanation of the parable of the sower in Mark 4:14 says, "The farmer sows the ***word***." The spoken and written Word of God are seeds of greatness.

Words are seeds with great power! Jesus said, "The words I have spoken to you are spirit, and they are life." John 6:63b

When you plant seeds of faith through the spoken word into your kid's ears, the guaranteed results will be seeds growing in their hearts producing a harvest of like kind! That's the reason it's so critically important ***what*** we speak to and over our children. It will produce a harvest! Are your words hope-giving or are they negative? Are they nourishing or destructive? Whichever they are will generate a harvest!

The nature of the seed is twofold: 1) to grow regardless of how tiny it begins, and 2) to grow into whatever kind it is. Small seeds - whatever kind they are - have the capacity to grow into something massive!

Here is another example of the seed. When we're born again, the incorruptible seed enters our spirits and makes us alive to God. The incorruptible seed is invisible, yet it causes everything in our lives to change. It takes time for the seed of Christ within us to grow but when it matures it has the capacity for 'great faith.'

The exciting thing about the seed is the potential existing within it from the beginning for incredible possibilities! "Being born again, not of corruptible seed, but of incorruptible, by the word of God, which liveth and abideth forever." I Peter 1:23 (KJV)

Jesus is referred to as the incarnate Word of God. "In the beginning was the Word, and the Word was with God, and the Word was God. The Word became flesh and made his dwelling among us…" John 1:1,14. Jesus Christ was planted in the womb of Mary as a seed through the power of the Holy Spirit and that seed changed history!

Let's remember, the only thing on planet earth with the capacity to grow is a seed! When we're born into this world we begin with a seed invisible to the naked eye. Yet, in that seed are all the components, genes, DNA, and molecular programming to develop its astonishing potential.

Faith begins very small but has no limits! How encouraging to kids and all of us to know, if we're born again, we all have faith no matter how minute. It is limitless in its capabilities. That's the message kids need to hear!

The basic principle then is, if you plant seed it will grow. We plant 'the seed' by speaking it. "…Behold a sower went forth to sow… when anyone *heareth* the word of the kingdom…" Matthew 13:3,19 (KJV)

The principle of the seed exists in all dimensions of life. Do you want to reap a harvest of corn? Plant corn. Do want to reap an abundance of money? Invest it. Do you want to have kids? Get married and experience intimacy. Do you want to be successful? Speak and listen to faith-filled word-seeds of who you are! Speak words of faith to kids and others and you will see powerful results!

THE 10th KEY TO SUCCESS MOTIVATION:

Give children problem-solving skills by instilling seeds of faith in them.

CHAPTER 11

THE DIFFERENCE BETWEEN CONTROL AND LEADERSHIP

Controllers are persons who through their insecurities, fears, or need for attention, try to manipulate people to get things to go their way. The Bible actually calls this a "work of the flesh." "The acts of the sinful nature are obvious:…idolatry and witchcraft…" Galatians 5:20a. The witchcraft listed here is not talking about occult witchcraft, it's talking about a work of "the sinful nature." Witchcraft is the total activation of the inward sinful desire toward attempting to get anything and everything we want. This is not a good thing. If everyone tried getting what they wanted all the time, we would live in a world of pandemonium and chaos.

We are seeing the consequences of witchcraft everyday more and more in our world.

It's in the DNA of kids and all of us to give in to the "witchcraft" within our nature. Have you noticed that? We were all born sinners with a craving for everyone and everything to conform to us. As children we have to learn hard lessons about sharing, forgiving, listening, and humility so we can make this world a better place. The inner desire for

Good and bad leadership happen everyday.

control is the reason we have strife, wars, crime, and troubles. That's why it's so critical for kids to understand true leadership.

I love to be in control! Don't you?

It feels good to be in charge! As a matter of fact, when I'm not in charge I tend to get fidgety and uncomfortable, but I've learned it's ok to let go.

Control can be a good thing and it can be a bad thing.

Have you ever come away from a party or some other gathering glad you're free from someone's control talk? Control talk can make you feel like nothing you say really matters. You probably don't intentionally plan get-togethers with that kind of person. That's the bad, negative kind of control.

Positive control on the other hand, is a good thing. Positive leadership is needed to bring order to a company, family, church, or nation. Someone needs to provide that direction and make good decisions in order to save a lot of grief and loss. To be effective, leaders must emerge and lead people! Control in our world is a must and is a good thing as long as it doesn't digress leaders into *'controllers.'* Teaching the 'right kind' of control is a critical component of success motivation.

Good and bad leadership happen everyday. Both good and bad leaders take control, the difference between the two is the center of focus. Bad leaders make decisions based on what is best for them. Bad leaders aren't really concerned about the good of all but only how their decisions will benefit them. Good leadership on the other hand, makes decisions based on what is best for the group or other people.

There's 'positive' control and there's 'negative' control. Negative control happens when someone takes charge who's not qualified, or when leaders are self appointed, or when they're in it for themselves and take advantage of others. Positive control provides protection, security, and benefit to those it serves.

I think we've all witnessed the abuse of controllers who are always telling people what to do, what to think, or where to go. They don't let others talk and make it known that only their view point matters. They're not fun to be around. They fall into the category of people who speak for everyone at a restaurant by telling the waitress, "No one is ordering dessert here because they're all fat."

What are the differences between a good leader and a controller? Being a good leader has less to do with being smart and more to do with being wise. There are so many issues we face everyday that make a huge difference to us on a practical level but they're not written anywhere in our legal system. Being kind instead of spiteful, being honest instead of deceitful, being fair instead of heavy handed. Kids who are given good examples develop into good leaders. Simply teaching leadership alone fails. Leadership must be clearly demonstrated by mentors and consistently walked out in front of kids.

The basis of true leadership is **moral strength**. Character is the ability for leaders to make right decisions in spite of pressure or the risk of personal loss. Right decisions might cost you popularity or reputation. A good

Being a good leader has less to do with being smart and more to do with being wise.

leader is willing to risk their popularity and reputation to follow their conscience and make the right decision.

In the Old Testament when King David was a young shepherd, he killed a bear and a lion to protect his father's sheep. He could have run away. He could have said, "I didn't sign up for this, too much risk!" He could have said, "What do a couple of sheep matter? My father will never know. I'll just turn my head instead of endangering my life."

That's not what David did. He cared about the sheep. He cared about his father's living, and he cared about keeping his word to watch the sheep. He killed the lion and the bear! In other words, **David had character!** That's inspiring! The Lord rejected the 7 other sons of Jesse and chose David to be king. Could it be the Lord looked at David's heart and not on the fact he was only a shepherd boy? That gives so much hope!

Preachers often find themselves in situations where compromising their convictions would benefit them. For example, it's tempting to allow the biggest donors in a congregation have the most influence over decision-making, even though the decisions may not be best for the people. The money these influential people give makes life easier for the pastor so *that* may be the reason behind why decisions are made, not because they're best for the church. A good pastor/leader doesn't give in to making decisions based on what's best for their pocket book, reputation, or popularity.

By the way - I'm sure you've noticed - bad politicians sell our nation, cities, or states "down the river" when it benefits them. They only make good decisions 'for the people' if it happens to benefit them. That's bad leadership. Good leadership goes beyond intelligence, experience, and eloquence and cares about the people they lead.

In contrast to evil politicians, Joseph, the 11th son of Jacob was sold into slavery by his brothers and went through years of arduous trials before he was promoted to vice Pharaoh of Egypt. It was quite a promotion since he became the second most powerful man on earth. He was taken from a wrongful 21-year prison sentence, a 'nobody' hidden away behind bars, and given the throne. Not only did he correctly interpret Pharaoh's dream (which none of the magicians or sorcerers could do) but he was honest, humble, patient, and God rewarded him.

Joseph dreamed a dream and God showed him seven years of plenty in Egypt and seven years of famine. He advised Pharoah to put someone in charge of storing the excess grain during the first seven year period to provide for the later years of famine. Since Joseph had displayed such great wisdom that exceeded the others, Pharoah put him in charge of all the grain production and storage as he suggested.

Joseph knew immediately what to do. He took control of all grain production in Egypt and began storing it. He possessed the insight and moral fortitude to plan for the famine before it arrived. He was in a position to benefit a lot of people and that's exactly what he did. His 'control' saved a nation.

Good leadership sees beforehand what's coming down the road, understands it and prepares for it. Poor, self-centered, or neglectful leadership doesn't worry about the danger coming. They "fight fires" when the problems arrive, managing one crises after another. This kind of leadership style is ego centered.

In contrast to Joseph, Jezebel, the wife of Ahab, King of Israel (875 B.C.) was a controller and a bad influence on the kingdom. She liked to dominate Ahab. She interfered in the all affairs of state and threatened the prophet Elijah for standing up against her evil. Her name is mentioned in the book of Revelation as a "seducer" and a "teacher of fornication." Not a pretty description. She came to a horrible fate at the end of her life when she was eaten by dogs (II

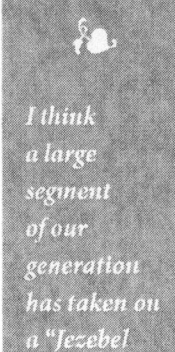

Kings 9:30-36). Those who have followed her ways are referred to in the Bible as those possessing a "spirit of Jezebel."

Where are the good leaders of today? I think a large segment of our generation has taken on a "Jezebel spirit." They don't listen. They have no respect. They want to be at the center of everything. They lie, flirt, exaggerate, threaten, and act out aggression and violence to gain control. They fake illness, pain, or give extreme reasons why they can't conform or produce anything.

These controllers slam doors, pout, scream, throw tantrums, and give others the silent treatment when they don't get their way. They manipulate conversations and threaten bizarre behavior to regain center stage. They rebel and speak evil of authority. They buckle under pressure and cause heartache and misery to their families and communities.

These are people without restraint. They have no class, no manners, and no consideration. They are the bully's of the world, the tyrants, the browbeaters, and the abusers. They want to rule and rise up in ascendancy. They want to be the master, not the servant. They live to domineer, hold sway, and otherwise take charge.

Where did they learn this? They learned this while they were young and impressionable. They learned while they were left to themselves. They learned this when no boundaries were set and parents weren't noticing. They spun out of control into self destruct mode because society told them there are no rules and therefore no consequences. Parents gave in. The child controllers of

> *I think a large segment of our generation has taken on a "Jezebel spirit."*

yesterday have become the tyrannical political leaders and dictators of today. They're arrogant, liberal thinkers, hypocrites, deceivers, and rebels.

Can you tell I feel passionate about this? In spite of this total vacuum of leadership, I have faith in this generation. Not all is lost. Not everyone has been influenced this way. Change is possible.

Let's go back to what good leadership looks like in the home. Do you think it's healthy for a child to pander for control and adulation all the time? Is it ok for a child to be given control just because he or she demands it or wants recognition for their slightest contribution? That's destructive!

It doesn't have to be that way!

Leaders lead best by developing the heart of a servant. They lead best when they listen to others. They lead best when they're aware of their own failure and brokenness, not by thinking they know it all. Leaders lead best by honoring others. They lead best by example and do not take the "do as I say but not as I do" approach. Good leadership happens when leaders recognize the value of input and the contribution of others.

I used to tell our church leadership team, "The only way we can come into agreement with one another is by discovering the areas in which we disagree, and that only happens if we talk to each other!" Talking requires humility because it assumes we don't have all the answers. Talking means someone is listening. Listening means the conversation is not one-sided.

When we take time to talk, we discover areas of

Leaders lead best by developing the heart of a servant.

disagreement with others. Everyone can benefit from this because collective ideas can be honed and refined and better solutions arrived at than if we try to come up with solutions all by ourselves. That's being smart and very mature.

In business, the type of environment that fosters acceptance is created by free and open discussion without the fear of intimidation. If everyone in a group is afraid of looking stupid or afraid of being cut off in the middle of a sentence by an overbearing leader, no one in the group is likely to speak up. This is true in families too. The group forfeits genuine agreement, new ideas are disregarded, and decision-making suffers.

It's liberating to realize you don't have to be right all the time. You don't always have to be in control. You can let someone else lead. In marriage, partners should take turns making decisions about little things and talk until they come into agreement about the big things. The 'best run' governments listen to the best ideas in spite of their origin but how rare is that? I encourage parents to give kids a voice when appropriate about what involves them. That kind of freedom will encourage their decision- making and thinking skills. If you genuinely give your kids a voice, they will make you the happiest parents alive! They will develop into fair, wise, and strong leaders.

Kids won't become controllers if they learn to take responsibility for their actions. They won't become controllers if they learn leadership is grounded in moral fortitude. They won't become controllers if they learn to

> *It's liberating to realize you don't have to be right all the time.*

care about others. Vince Lombardi once said, "If you're going to play together as a team, you've got to care for one another. You've go to love each other."

Dynamic leaders grow in an atmosphere which values **what's right** not **who's right.**

As youth listen to others and express their ideas they can change the world. They will succeed because they're not threatened by ideas better than their own. This kind of freedom will enable them to flourish because their ideas are then considered, respected, and followed.

THE 11th KEY TO SUCCESS MOTIVATION:

Differentiate between control and leadership.

CHAPTER 12

EMBRACING FORGIVENESS

Kids are little people and need forgiveness like the rest of us. When I was involved with my kid's everyday activities, time seemed to stop. I thought they would never grow up. It seemed like they made a hundred mistakes everyday and that was hard to take.

Then it occurred to me.

The stage on which the drama of their lives was being acted out would never have a final curtain call! There was always going to be something! Kids will always be making mistakes – they're kids. Though, as they grow, hopefully they make fewer and fewer because someone is taking the time to gently correct them and show them a better way. Good news! Making mistakes is o.k.! I learned to forgive them and helped them forgive themselves. I taught them to make better choices! Now they're on their own. Some of their decisions have been good ones, some not so good. That's alright. I can look back and honestly say it was well worth my investment of time and effort to lead them into forgiveness – of themselves and others. I pointed out to them if they wanted to receive forgiveness, they must humbly first give it to others.

Parents ought to remind themselves, "My kids won't be around forever." I don't own them and won't be making decisions for them when they're gone. I need to forgive them and teach them to forgive themselves and others." If parents forgive their kids, then they've figured out the way for them to grow into emotionally healthy adults. Allowing kids to make their own decisions as they grow means parents must forgive them. It means parents must continue to believe in them after they fail. Forgiveness allows kids to learn autonomy. It allows healthy decision-making even though kids don't always get it right and may get bruised in the process of their own decision-making.

Of course, decision-making should be age appropriate. Kids may not know how to make good financial decisions about adult spending issues, but they **can** certainly learn to make good decisions about their weekly allowance.

By the way, I want to point out here, many decisions parents make for their children I want to call 'non-negotiable.' Why?

Let's face reality. Kids are confronted with many temptations today they're not able to resist if given too much freedom. Kids cannot lead themselves. They're kids. They can't make good decisions about important stuff of their lives unless they're taught.

It's up to parents to make critical decisions for their kids while they're growing up that include becoming involved in a Christian church, dating, attendance at a private or public school, the age they're allowed to drive a car, modesty, and handling money, to name a few. Only parents can make these decisions. If parents don't step to the plate and make these decisions but abdicate them to

> *Parents ought to remind themselves, "My kids won't be around forever."*

someone else instead, they are flinging their kids' future to chance, and *"**the chance kids will make it without parents' intervention doesn't exist.**"*

I know the following are strong words but I feel compelled to say them. If parents don't make a deliberate, thoughtful, specific, exerted, and persistent effort to find a gospel preaching church and get their kids involved in children's ministry, youth ministry, and adult worship for themselves and for their kids, they are literally throwing their kids to the hellish and fiendish schemes of Satan who will rule over them. Satan is not a friend. He doesn't love us and he doesn't care the age of the person he wants to obliterate. He will lie, steal, and devastate. That's who he is. He will bring untold damage to the lives of your children if you remain passive in your role in their spiritual development. Satan will take them down.

Let me emphasize - involvement in church today is a 100% and absolute utter necessity for you and your children. It cannot be cast aside or treated casually. Does that mean churches and pastors are perfect? Does it mean you won't have issues with the church you attend? No, there will always be issues with the very best of circumstances. Better an imperfect church than no church at all! If I make up my mind to be critical, I can find something wrong with almost anything. I had to stop doing that! There was a point in my life I had to come against the bad attitudes and decide once and for all I was going to be positive, faith-filled, and happy no matter what.

Wake up parents! Listen to the voice of wisdom, experience, and truth. Do you really expect your kids to somehow miraculously make it when the heat is being turned up in every aspect of their lives? We're facing massive problems in our nation and world - political, moral, societal, natural disasters, monetary crises and leadership crises in high places. You must be intentional about being committed to a church fellowship. It's not an option! Don't make the mistake of ignoring or treating it lightly!

If parents today do not make a deliberate plan to get their kids involved in spiritual growth, the enemy of their souls will accommodate the vacuum and they will be snatched away by a corrupt culture that is becoming more powerful and destructive everyday.

Be encouraged. Parenting is not easy. It's not easy to see your kids as competent, capable, and adept when they're growing up, **but they are becoming what you're planting in them.**

When my kids were growing up, I couldn't see much progress in their maturity. I had to get perspective! Now that they're grown, I look back now and say, "They were gone in a flash!" We need to guard against treating our kids like possessions or pawns to be used however we choose. We should not speak to them in demeaning ways or treat them harshly. Children are people in small packages. Treat them with respect. Treat them gently. Treat them as you would a friend – kindly – and yet as those needing your direction, discipline, wisdom, and understanding.

It's important for kids to learn not to judge others with harshness or condemnation. Your opportunity to teach them will abound! Stay tuned, I guarantee

> *It's important for kids to learn not to judge others with harshness or condemnation.*

examples of how not to judge will come up often. I chose to use my own mistakes as illustrations to help my kids. They now have an ample supply of memories of what not to do by looking at me! I was particularly rigid and strict in my youth and in a hurry to judge everyone. I've since learned a better way and hope I imparted that to them.

I shared the following story with my kids as an example of judging. It's about a road trip my wife and I took in Southern California.

We had been on the road for what seemed like hours and evening was finally falling. As the darkness fully set in, I reached for the headlights. I pulled but nothing happened. No headlights! We were startled beyond words.

Here we were, in the middle of nowhere, it was dark, and we had no light. There were no mechanics, no gas stations, and no stores anywhere for miles and miles. What were we going to do? I turned the switch on and off and on and off again. Nothing. Then I tried the high beams. The high beams were working! We had light! Lots of it! That was great until we met an oncoming car. The other cars would flash their high beams feverishly to signal us to lower ours. I couldn't respond. I decided that flashing my lights would be dangerous since they would go dark, and that might distract, scare, or annoy the other car so I just sat there helplessly watching them go by. My wife and I thought they must have been pretty ticked off because we never turned off our high beams. More often than not, oncoming cars signaling to turn off our high beams ended up leaving their high beams on. We figured this was most likely other drivers acting out their frustration or maybe punishing us for our 'lack of consideration.'

That experience taught us a valuable lesson we passed on to our kids. When you're driving and someone doesn't lower their high beams, it could mean they don't have any low beams. Instead of getting miffed and saying a few choice words, try understanding. Maybe they have no low beams. Forgive them. This could be applied to countless scenarios.

Why is reserving judgment such a critical lesson for kids to learn? Judging others sets the 'judge' up as inspector, not a friend. Do you want to be your neighbor's inspector? Judging sets up the judge to be right and everyone else wrong. Do you want to be Mr. district attorney on the block, your church, or your kid's school? That's not a good thing. Behind the premise of judging is the assumption that we have special insight. It's the assumption we are in fact judges. It's those assumptions that give us pride in ourselves because "we're never guilty for the same thing."

We are no one's judge.

Jesus said, "Do not judge, or you too will be judged." Matthew 7:1 Judging is God's job, not ours. If we make a habit of condemning others, kids will pick up on it in a New York minute and assume they also have the right to do the same.

"Don't judge." Actually, that statement is quite liberating. When I finally realized it wasn't my place to judge, what a relief! I stopped equating my personal opinions as gospel truth and stopped storing up grievances to unload on someone when they "did something to annoy me again."

Does this mean we never make judgments? No. Making judgments is an important part of our daily lives. It's critical to be wise and avoid pitfalls. There are two kinds of judgment, 'condemning' and 'discerning.'

Judging is God's job, not ours.

TWO KINDS OF JUDGMENT: *Condemning and Discerning*

> *Freely forgiving is essential to a calm life.*

The word 'condemn in Webster's Dictionary means to "inflict a penalty upon, to doom, to declare unfit for use." Stay away from that kind of judgment! It elevates and arrogates persons to demigods. At the end of the day, judgment is reserved for God alone. Is it the Lord's heart to condemn us? No. The Bible says, "For God did not send his Son into the world to condemn the world, but to save the world through him." John 3:17 It's God's intention to save us from condemnation, not subject us to it. We need to follow His example by not condemning others.

I used to tell members of our congregation, "Don't gossip and talk about things before you have all the facts. When you have all the facts, only talk to the parties involved. Ask yourself, "Do I have any real evidence about what and why this is happening?" If you don't, you have no right to trash a reputation based on an emotional reaction to some action on their part.

There are so many aspects to the actions of others. Let's be honest and admit we're not equipped with enough information or details to understand. Even if we were, we've not been set up over them to condemn.

Discerning judgment - in contrast to condemning judgment - is different. It means to determine rightly, esteem, estimate, and correctly surmise without passing a sentence upon someone. All of us need discerning judgment every day of our lives!

Discerning judgment is wise judgment with the stinger

of condemnation removed. We're called to awaken and not be naïve. We're called not to let the wool be pulled over our eyes. We're called to open our eyes to the difference between right and wrong.

Children need a balanced approach of deciding for themselves what is right and wrong without slapping a penalty on everyone who disagrees with them. We are supposed to live knowing what is right without criticizing and chiding everyone who disagrees with us. I used to teach my kids the 'forgiveness triangle.'

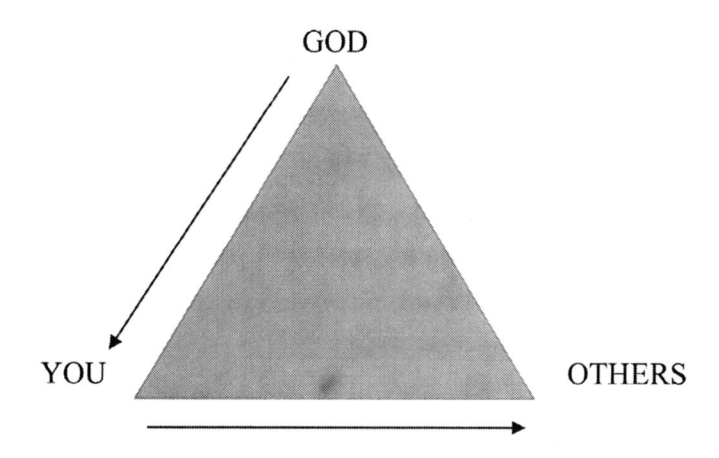

```
                    GOD


        YOU                    OTHERS
```

God is at the top, you are at one corner, and others are at the opposite end. The Bible says if we don't forgive others, (horizontally across the bottom line of the triangle) then God will not forgive us! (Vertically down from the top). "…if you forgive not men their trespasses, neither will your Father forgive your trespasses." Matthew 6:15 By the way, how could anyone not forgive someone else when all of us do the same things, just in a different way?

Freely forgiving is essential to a calm life. If you want to be stress free, forgive. If you want to live a long, healthy life, learn to forgive. If you don't want to grow into a bitter, resentful, grouchy old cynic, then forgive. Abundant medical research shows bitterness is the cause of a very long list of physical diseases.

Wouldn't it be great if kids could be taught it's not their place to hold court on everyone? Wouldn't it be great if kids could learn to hold back judgment, be patient, and not jump to conclusions? Wouldn't it be great if kids could hold their tongues and show compassion? Well, they can! We'd all live a lot happier life and maybe even longer if we could learn how to release others, not condemn them.

Let's show mercy. Let's Pardon. Let's grant Amnesty. When we do, we'll find mercy and pardon coming our way. "…judgment without mercy will be shown to anyone who has not been merciful. Mercy triumphs over judgment!" James 2:12. Whenever I'm asked, "What is the greatest thing that ever happened to you? I say, "Forgiveness!!"

Teach kids to forgive and they will grow up into kind, whole, wise, and motivated adults!

May God's abundant blessing rest upon you, my reader. May you now become a teacher of success motivation to everyone you meet.

THE 12th KEY TO SUCCESS MOTIVATION:

Guide children into forgiveness

CHILDREN'S BILL OF RIGHTS

Children have a right to:

- #1 love themselves
- #2 g-r-o-w u-p slowly
- #3 be respected as human beings
- #4 be seen *and* heard
- #5 not be compared to other children or siblings
- #6 be forgiven
- #7 be allowed to fail
- #8 be given more praise than criticism
- #9 be given spiritual values
- #10 be endowed with opportunities to develop their God-given gifts

THE 12 KEYS TO SUCCESS MOTIVATION:

#1 Lead children into unconditionally accepting themselves.

#2 Impart self value to kids with words, actions, and affection.

#3 Accept yourself as a parent and love your children based on the free gift of love from God.

#4 Teach children the true origin of authority and how to use it.

#5 Model and impart 'good' authority to kids.

#6 Give kids good, positive, and measured discipline.

#7 Take on humility and teach it to your children.

#8 Affirm children's ideas.

#9 Give freedom to kids at the right time.

#10 Give children problem-solving skills by instilling seeds of faith in them.

#11 Differentiate between control and leadership.

#12 Guide children into forgiveness.

KEN'S KIDS

∽

I _am_ a proud dad. I deeply love all three of my kids and miss them everyday they're away from me. The following overview is kind of like the 'proof of the pudding' side of <u>Success Motivation</u>. It's the answer to the question, "How did his kids turn out? By the way, there is so much more to them than these mere facts!

Robby   My first son, born January 20, 1974
       Married Melissa Snyder, currently residing in Oklahoma City, Oklahoma. Their 3 boys: Kenny, Rylind, & Kaedin

2006-present

　***Vice President**, Advanced Network Design, Oklahoma City, OK,

2006

　***Network Engineer**, Mid-Atlantic Operations Midwest Research Institute, Washington, D.C.1999-2006

　***Network Manager**, State of Oklahoma, Indigent Defense Systems, Oklahoma City, OK1999-present

*Second Lieutenant, United States Air Force, 137th Communication Flight 2003

*Bachelor of Science – Business E-Business & Information Systems

*Devoted Christian, father, and husband, serving in ministry at his local church

****

Ryan   My second son, born May 8, 1976
             Residing in Sacramento, California

2009-present

***Captain, United States Air Force**, "RQ-4 Global Hawk Pilot/ Mission

Beale AFB. CA Commander"

2006-2009

***Global Hawk Operations Center Supervisor,** Responsible for coordinating priorities with Joint Air Operations Centers worldwide

2004-2006

***Central Flight Scheduler and Aircrew Manager,** in command of 10 crew members in mission to meet the Secretary of Defense, Joint Chiefs of Staff and Unified Command Intelligence needs worldwide.

2004

*derecho**Bachelor of Arts in Government/Political Science**

*derecho**Strong Christian serving as lead guitarist on church worship team.**

****

Alison   My first and only daughter, born October 7, 1981
Married to Ryan Bestelmeyer, residing in Long Beach, CA
Their daughter and son: Aubrey & Aaron

2009 –present

*Gave birth to her beautiful daughter Aubrey and son Aaron

*Serves twice a month at a shelter for homeless, pregnant women

*Involved in leadership positions at church

2005-2009

*Middle School teacher in Long Beach, CA

*Received "Mustang Pride Award" recognizing outstanding service and dedication to students

2004-2005

*Earned Professional Clear Teaching Credential

2003

*Bachelor of Arts in Liberal Studies

*Caring mom, wife, and passionate Christian leader serving alongside her husband in college ministry where he is pastor

****

NOTES

Author contact information: kenteel@yahoo.com